TO MY DEAR FRIEND:

FROM:

Journey to the Cross

Journey to the Cross

FORTY DAYS TO PREPARE YOUR HEART FOR EASTER

(in)courage editor
Mary Carver

B&H
PUBLISHING
NASHVILLE, TENNESSEE

Published by B&H Publishing Group
Nashville, Tennessee

Dewey Decimal Classification: 242.34
Subject Heading: EASTER / LENT / DEVOTIONAL LITERATURE

Style guide by Emily Strnad. Design and illustration by Katherine
Hamm. Additional design and hand lettering by Jennifer Tucker.

1 2 3 4 5 6 7 • 24 23 22 21 20

CONTENTS

LENT CALENDAR

The *Journey to the Cross* Experience begins on Ash Wednesday and proceeds through the next 40 days, *not including Sundays*, leading up to Easter Sunday.

Use the Lent Calendar provided here to help you keep track of the days. Once you've completed each day's reading, check the box provided to keep track of your progress.

TAKEAWAYS FROM THIS LENT SEASON

As you move through the next 40 days, use the lines below to keep track of the biggest lessons God has taught you.

S	M	T	W	T	F	S
			DAY 1 ☐ Ash Wednesday	DAY 2 ☐	DAY 3 ☐	DAY 4 ☐
	DAY 5 ☐	DAY 6 ☐	DAY 7 ☐	DAY 8 ☐	DAY 9 ☐	DAY 10 ☐
	DAY 11 ☐	DAY 12 ☐	DAY 13 ☐	DAY 14 ☐	DAY 15 ☐	DAY 16 ☐
	DAY 17 ☐	DAY 18 ☐	DAY 19 ☐	DAY 20 ☐	DAY 21 ☐	DAY 22 ☐
	DAY 23 ☐	DAY 24 ☐	DAY 25 ☐	DAY 26 ☐	DAY 27 ☐	DAY 28 ☐
	DAY 29 ☐	DAY 30 ☐	DAY 31 ☐	DAY 32 ☐	DAY 33 ☐	DAY 34 ☐
Palm Sunday	DAY 35 ☐	DAY 36 ☐	DAY 37 ☐	DAY 38 ☐	DAY 39 ☐ Good Friday	DAY 40 ☐

Quiet Time

Immediately the Spirit drove him into the wilderness. He was in the wilderness forty days, being tempted by Satan. He was with the wild animals, and the angels were serving him.

MARK 1:12–13

I'm sitting at my dining room table, country music playing just a smidge too loud behind me as my daughters have a dance party on what feels like the seventy-third snow day this month. I reach for my Bible, running my hand down the whisper-thin pages, and close my eyes.

Before I can even say hello to God, much less reflect on His holiness, one of my daughters is crying and the other is shouting about how it's not her fault, she didn't do anything! This time, I close my eyes, but in frustration, not reverence.

I settle this latest argument and suggest a litany of quiet activities my kids might enjoy for a while. Finally, peace. My hand hovers over my Bible, but—much as I'm embarrassed to admit it—I hesitate. My phone is sitting right there, just waiting for me, begging for my attention, promising to entertain me and numb all the irritations that have cropped up this day.

Even if I manage to ignore the pull of my phone, my mind and heart are still so prone to wander.

What time is my appointment this afternoon?

Did I return that message? I should do that real quick, right now.

Why is the cat crying? Guess I better give her fresh water.

That reminds me: I need to refill my water bottle.

Maybe I should try that devotional I bought a few months ago.

I'm just going to pay that bill online . . . and answer that one email . . . and check on that project . . .

When I began studying ways to prepare my heart for Easter, something many know as the season of Lent, I read everything I could find about the time Jesus spent in the wilderness. While accounts can be found in three of the Gospels, the brief description in Mark is what resonated most deeply with me.

Thinking of Jesus, alone in the wilderness, being tempted by Satan, and surrounded by wild animals was a breath of fresh air to my distracted, weary soul. I feel alone! I'm tempted all the time! And yes, at times it feels like I'm surrounded by wild animals!

When we struggle to quiet our lives and our hearts enough to focus on God, Jesus knows exactly how we feel. And what I know from passages in Matthew and Luke is that, despite the desperate situation in which He found Himself, He resisted temptation. The angels served Him, He leaned on His knowledge of Scripture and faith in God, and He resisted.

So what does that mean for me, as I think about one more failed attempt at a simple quiet time? What does that mean for you, as you feel the hunger and isolation of wilderness or battle attacks from temptation of all kinds? As you long for communion with the Lord but feel unable to get there, to stay there, to remember why you were going there in the first place?

It means this: our Lord and Savior isn't just the One who can quench our thirst and ease our pain. He is worthy of our praise and adoration, but He also is intimately familiar with our challenges and our struggles. He knows the strength it requires to seek Him and abide with Him, and He knows that, without Him, we will perish in the wilderness.

Not only is Jesus our GOAL when we set aside time for Him, He is our SOLUTION for fighting through all the distractions + temptations that work so hard to keep us away.

It means that not only is Jesus our goal when we set aside time for Him, He is our solution for fighting through all the distractions and temptations that work so hard to keep us away. It means that, no matter how barren and empty our personal wilderness may feel, we are not actually alone in our search for God. Just as the angels were with Him, Jesus is with us.

Dear Lord, thank You for going first into the wilderness—for showing us how important it is to get alone and quiet, to seek God, and to listen. Thank You for going with us when we face temptation and distraction—for giving us the tools we need to resist. Jesus, You are worth every effort it takes to quiet my mind and my heart. You are worthy of every minute I devote to You above all else. Please meet me in this place. Bind my wandering heart to Yours. Keep my eyes set on You. Thank You, Lord, for never letting me go. Amen.

QUESTIONS TO CONSIDER

1. Do you find it difficult to consistently spend time with God?

_____

_____

_____

_____

_____

_____

2. Is the biggest challenge to a regular quiet time an external distraction or an internal one?

_____

_____

_____

_____

_____

_____

3. What is one way you can sit with God today, if even for a few minutes?

_____

_____

_____

_____

_____

_____

_____

_____

_____

_____

_____

_____

DAY 2
REFLECTION

We all know Easter as a celebration of Jesus' resurrection—the day He conquered death for us all and rose from the dead. Given how important this day is, preparing for Easter is something Christians have done for thousands of years.

Many know this season of preparation as Lent, the forty weekdays from Ash Wednesday to Holy Saturday, all leading up to resurrection Sunday. During this time, believers around the world reflect, repent, and pray as a way to prepare their hearts for Easter.

What does Lent mean to you?

Have you observed Lent before? What did that look like for you?

Why have you chosen to prepare your heart for Easter this year?

_____

_____

_____

What do you hope will be different when we reach Easter?

_____

_____

_____

How will you make the next forty days different than every other day of the year?

_____

_____

_____

How do you plan to set aside extra time for the Lord during this season of preparation?

_____

_____

_____

Outdoorsy

LORD, our Lord,
how magnificent is your name throughout the earth!
You have covered the heavens with your majesty.
From the mouths of infants and nursing babies,
you have established a stronghold
on account of your adversaries
in order to silence the enemy and the avenger.
When I observe your heavens,
the work of your fingers,
the moon and the stars,
which you set in place,
what is a human being that you remember him,
a son of man that you look after him?
You made him little less than God
and crowned him with glory and honor.
You made him ruler over the works of your hands;
you put everything under his feet:
all the sheep and oxen,

as well as the animals in the wild,
the birds of the sky,
and the fish of the sea
that pass through the currents of the seas.
LORD, our Lord,
how magnificent is your name throughout the earth!

PSALM 8

I'm not what you'd call an outdoorsy person. In fact you'd be accurate to call me an indoorsy person. No matter the season or the weather, I prefer air conditioning and carpet far more than fresh air and green grass.

But that doesn't mean my soul doesn't crave interactions with the outdoors. It does, but I don't always realize it until I'm forced outside and catch an unexpected glimpse of God's creation.

If I'm not careful, I can spend all my days with my head down—staring at a screen or the work of my hands, focused on the immediate and the urgent, ignoring what's going on outside my reach, my home, my small world. Without realizing it, I've secured blinders on my face and my heart, filtering out most of the world and, as a result, most of the One who made that world.

Thank God for brilliant sunsets and blizzards and views from an airplane window. Thank God for puppies and people with different perspectives and all the big and small ways His creation breaks the monotony of the everyday and reminds me just how big this world is (and how He is infinitely bigger than that).

Thank God
for all the
big and small ways
His creation breaks the
monotony of my every day
and reminds me
just how BIG this world is
(and how He is infinitely
bigger than that).

My husband and I have an ongoing debate. We both love the mountains and, in particular, have really enjoyed time we've spent in Colorado. We find the magnitude and beauty of the mountains to be breathtaking and humbling and an undeniable testimony to God's greatness. We find that our eyes are drawn to the natural beauty whether we're hiking to a waterfall or driving through crowded streets. Up close or in the distance, the mountains refuse to be ignored and keep us mindful of God at all times.

The debate comes in when we imagine living near such natural beauty. If mountains were simply part of our everyday environment, would we remain so focused on their magnificence and their creator? Would we be able to maintain a posture of wonder and worship, or would we eventually put the blinders back on?

One of us (hint: it's me) insists that I would never tire of gazing at the mountains in gratitude and awe. I can't imagine a world in which I don't even notice the towering peaks and swooping valleys. Surely they would never become normal or grow old; surely I'd never stop hearing the call of nature and crave its message of God's power and love.

Except . . . this is exactly what happens nearly every day of my life. I stop to breathe in the fresh air. I stare at the bright pinks and oranges striping the sky, blinking away tears of gratitude for such a show. I smile at the calves in the field as I speed down the highway. And then I go about my life, head down, eyes back on the immediate and the urgent, forgetting once again the splendor of this world and the song it sings of God's glory.

Can you relate? Do you find it easier to keep your head down than to look up and out at the world God created? Could you use a reminder to pause and observe the heavens and the works of God's hands?

What a difference it might make if we regularly let nature point us to God! What a different perspective we might have when we look back at our small corner of the world, after contemplating the vastness of the world He's made!

As we move toward the time for remembering Christ's sacrifice and resurrection, the ultimate act of love, let's also set aside time to remember God's creativity and power in making the world, the original act of love. After all, the world Jesus came to save had to be made first, and God decided to make it beautiful. Let's watch the mountains point to the heavens and listen to the seas roar His name. Let's look up and remember who He is and how powerful He is. Let's never grow tired of hearing His creation shout the magnificence of His name.

Heavenly Father, I am in awe of You. When I see the mountains or a rushing river, a flower pushing its way out of the ground or a sunset painting the sky, I cannot deny that You are a mighty and powerful God. You are a wonderful artist, and I'm so grateful. Thank You, Lord, for giving us beauty in every corner of this planet—to enjoy but, more important, to remind us of your magnificence. Forgive me, God, for the days I never look up once, for the times I'm so focused on myself that I forget to look for You. Please keep reminding me, keep pulling my eyes up. Don't let me get tired of or used to the wonder of You. Help me see the beauty of the world You came to save. I love You. Thank You. Amen.

QUESTIONS TO CONSIDER

1. Can you think of a time you were overwhelmed by God's creativity and power while spending time outdoors?

_____

_____

_____

_____

_____

2. What part of God's creation most reminds you of Him?

_____

_____

_____

_____

3. How can you find time to appreciate God's goodness in nature today?

_____

_____

_____

_____

DAY 4
PSALM 98

Sing a new song to the Lord, for he has
    performed wonders;
his right hand and holy arm have won him victory.
The Lord has made his victory known;
he has revealed his righteousness in the sight of
    the nations.
He has remembered his love and faithfulness to the
    house of Israel;
all the ends of the earth have seen our
    God's victory.

Let the whole earth shout to the Lord; be jubilant,
    shout for joy, and sing.
Sing to the Lord with the lyre, with the lyre and
    melodious song.
With trumpets and the blast of the ram's horn
shout triumphantly in the presence of the
    Lord, our King.

Let the sea and all that fills it, the world and those
    who live in it, resound.
Let the rivers clap their hands;
let the mountains shout together for joy before the
    Lord, for he is coming to judge the earth.
He will judge the world righteously and the
    peoples fairly.

DAY 5
DEVOTION

Facing Sin

In the year that King Uzziah died, I saw the Lord seated on a high and lofty throne, and the hem of his robe filled the temple. Seraphim were standing above him; they each had six wings: with two they covered their faces, with two they covered their feet, and with two they flew. And one called to another:

Holy, holy, holy is the Lord of Armies;
his glory fills the whole earth.

The foundations of the doorways shook at the sound of their voices, and the temple was filled with smoke.

Then I said:

Woe is me for I am ruined
because I am a man of unclean lips
and live among a people of unclean lips,
and because my eyes have seen the King,
the Lord of Armies.

Then one of the seraphim flew to me, and in his hand was a glowing coal that he had taken from the altar with tongs. He touched my mouth with it and said:

Now that this has touched your lips,
your iniquity is removed
and your sin is atoned for.

ISAIAH 6:1–7

Though the imagery used in the book of Isaiah is incredibly vivid, I've never quite been able to picture such a fantastic scenario. Strangely enough, a TV show I recently watched made it much more clear.

Jane is a television character who used to be a "bad guy" but is now a "good guy" with limited memories of the person she used to be. When she began facing the horrible deeds she'd committed in her past but had previously forgotten, she admitted:

"I don't know if I can do this. I thought I could close the door on my past, quarantine it, but I can't. . . . I'm so tired. I'm tired of fighting, tired of trying, tired of remembering. I just want to forget."

Later, she confessed to a counselor how overwhelmed she was by the things she's done: "There are so many of them, too many to atone for. I don't even know where to begin. And when I think about it, it just completely paralyzes me."

Fortunately, I've never committed murder or treason or any of the many truly horrible things this fictional character had done. I'm guessing you haven't either.

But I still know how she feels.

Recently, I've been reading a book with a women's small group at my church, and it's caused me to have a few "Jane" (or Isaiah) moments of my own. The book we're reading is about sharing Jesus with the people in your life; and as we've been reading chapter after chapter, I've been challenged in how I view—and treat—people. I've been motivated to live a little differently, to listen a little more intently to what the Lord has likely been trying to tell me for a while. But more than that, reading this book has brought to mind, and heart, several times I have seriously hurt people.

I've remembered so many instances where, despite knowing what God's Word says about loving my neighbor, I did the exact opposite. I've remembered times when I wasn't just distant or negligent, but also times when I was intentionally hurtful. I've remembered a whole lot of things I had previously swept under the carpet of my memory, things I've never reckoned with or confessed.

So while I have very little in common with Jane on the surface, I know exactly how she feels.

I know how it feels to be so convinced I was in the right or that nobody got hurt and it was fine. I think, *It's over. We all need to just get over it.* I know how it feels to be so certain of those things that I completely forget about what I actually said or did.

And I know how it feels to be blindsided by a memory that I'd stuffed down so deep that part of me believes it never happened. I know how it feels to be gobsmacked by the realization that I was the one in the wrong, that what I said or did (or didn't say or didn't do) was a really big deal. I know how Jane feels when the pain she'd caused and the shame she now feels rush over her in waves until she can't breathe.

And just like Isaiah, I know how it feels to be confronted with the overwhelming goodness of the Almighty God at the same time I'm breathtakingly cognizant of my own failure and fallibility. The gap between His perfection and my brokenness is just too wide to bridge. The valley between us is just too deep to cross. I wouldn't even know where to start.

Do you know how that feels?

I don't know if I can do this.

I just want to forget.

There are too many sins to atone for.

I don't know where to begin.

It's true. We can't do this. We can't atone for all our sins. And, unfortunately, forgetting forever isn't really an option. But unlike Jane, we are not left hopeless in the face of our reckoning and realizations. We are not left alone to try to fight and work until we collapse under the weight of our humanity. No, we are not hopeless, and we are not alone.

We have Jesus.

Like Isaiah, we have the immeasurable grace of God that offers mercy and forgiveness despite our undeniable depravity. We have the ultimate sacrifice of Christ that means atonement is attainable after all. And we have the unbeatable strength of our Lord, who promises to never leave us, even when we do unspeakable things.

We cannot bear the burden of our sins, and we cannot erase them from history or repair the damage they've done. But it's okay. We were never

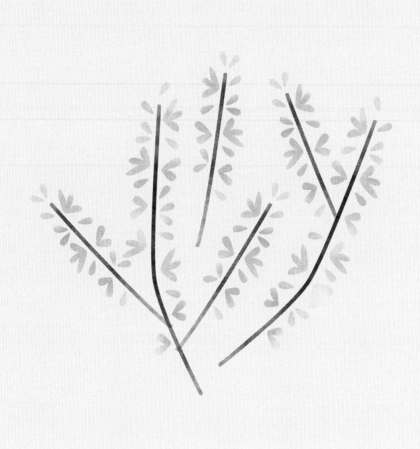

meant to. God has given us a way to face our past, our sins, ourselves. He has given us a way to heal and to move forward. Jesus is the place we begin and the place our sins come to an end. He is the one who looks at everything we are and everything we've done—even, and especially, the parts we've tried to hide—and He says, "You are loved. You are forgiven. It is finished."

If you're breaking under the weight of your sin today,

If you're afraid to face the reality of what has gone before,

If you don't know how you can possibly handle this, how you can ever move on,

I pray God will open your eyes to the ultimate truth, to the gift of salvation, to the forgiveness and atonement that we all desperately need. I pray that He will hold you close and comfort you when you grieve, that He will give you strength and resilience and guidance as you move forward. I pray you will no longer feel exhausted or terrified or paralyzed, that you will accept the gift He's offering you and walk forward with eyes open and heart full.

Because you are loved. You are forgiven. It is finished.

God, You are so mighty and powerful and good. You are perfect. You are holy. And, Lord, I am not. I am so far from holy or good that at times it feels like I can't even see good—or You—from here. When I face the things I've done, I'm overwhelmed with grief and shame, and I don't know how I can ever face You. But You are so kind and gracious and merciful, Lord. You know just how very human I am, and yet You reach out to me anyway. You offer me the biggest and best gift of all: forgiveness. And You give me the strength to accept that forgiveness and move forward. You have done the work that I can't do; You have paid the price for my sins. For that I am eternally grateful. Thank You, God. Thank You so much. I love You. Amen.

QUESTIONS TO CONSIDER

1. Have you ever forgotten a mistake or sin, only to remember it later? Or have you ever been convinced you were right, only to realize later how completely wrong you were? Who did you hurt? What was that like?

2. When the burden of your sin feels too heavy to bear, how are you tempted to respond? Do you try to forget? Do you try to pay for it yourself? Do you deflect or make light of it? Or do you react some other way? Why do you think this is your typical response to your sin?

---

3. What do you need to ask God's forgiveness for during this Lent season? What is weighing you down and keeping you from experiencing the freedom Jesus offers?

DAY 6
GRATITUDE QUOTE

*"Gratitude is an offering precious
in the sight of God, and it is one that
the poorest of us can make and be not
poorer but richer for having made it."*

—A. W. TOZER, *LEADERSHIP: JOY OR BURDEN*

As we carve out extra time to spend connecting with the Lord during Lent, let us start with gratitude. Ask Him to open your eyes to the many ways He's blessed you, even in hard seasons or difficult times. Ask Him to keep you mindful of His power and might, His love and care, His grace and mercy. Take a moment each day to write down the gifts He's given you and why you're so thankful.

DAY 7
DEVOTION

Renovation

Dear friends, we are God's children now, and what we will be has not yet been revealed. We know that when he appears, we will be like him because we will see him as he is. And everyone who has this hope in him purifies himself just as he is pure.

1 JOHN 3:2–3

I read her text message and smiled. Sometimes you tell a friend about a struggle and that friend listens, offers some advice, maybe even prays for you, and then never mentions it again. Other friends do all that—but then call a week later to see if you've made any progress.

I'd told my friend about how overwhelmed I'm feeling in this season and about how my frustration stems from recognizing the necessity of saying "no" but not knowing how. She texted me several days later to ask if I'd identified the things I need to let go of in my schedule, as well as the things I need to keep in it. I gave her a simple, surface-level answer that also made it clear that I was still struggling. Some friends would have left it at that. But this friend pushed back one more time, asking if I'd taken action in a specific way we'd discussed.

"Have you made a list, so you can see everything you do on one piece of paper?"

I left that message unread on my phone for days. I didn't respond. But I wasn't ignoring her. I was simply waiting until I'd done the thing, until I'd figured something out, until I wasn't such a mess before talking to my friend.

Rather than admit I'd spent more than an hour staring at half a dozen pieces of paper torn from a legal pad and covered in ink as I tried to wrap my mind and a pen around all the responsibilities and opportunities I'm facing right now, I stayed silent. Instead of confessing that the longer I looked at those words, the more overwhelmed I got until the prospect of making a simple to-do list (normally one of my favorite things, honestly) drove me to tears, I refused to answer.

I didn't want her to see how undone I was. Not until I'd figured it out, cleaned it up, gotten it together. Then it would be okay to tell the story of that one time I lost my mind over a to-do list. But right then, while I was in the worst of the procrastination and fear? No way. Nobody needs to see that.

Then a few weeks ago, I noticed a house in our neighborhood that was falling apart. More than a cracked driveway or peeling paint, this was major disintegration at a rapid rate. And I was super annoyed to see it.

As I drove by that first day, I felt my nose wrinkle and my lip curl in disgust. I assumed that the house in question was simply being neglected, although perhaps it had been completely abandoned. Either way, the lack of attention and care being given the home bothered me—enough that I actually drove a block out of my way to avoid seeing it.

Over the next few days, I realized that someone was actually rehabbing this house. The tearing down was intentional, and a building up was surely coming soon. Strangely enough, that wasn't enough for this judgmental neighbor. Even though I knew this house was in the process of transformation, I still felt my lip curl as I glanced toward the siding-less house with the overgrown weeds. I did think, with some curiosity, *Huh. So that's what a house looks like under siding.* But my response to that thought was immediate and dismissive: *Gross.*

I know myself. When the work on that house is finished, I'll be genuinely delighted. On the day I drive by and see a brand-new, beautiful house standing where a pile of wood stood just a few weeks prior, I will be genuinely impressed by my neighbor's hard work and commitment to improving their home.

And yet, while I know I can only truly appreciate the "after" picture in comparison to the "before" shot, I really did not want to witness the in-between. And though I say that I appreciate a homeowner's labor of love involved in rehabbing a house, the truth is, I didn't actually want to see the mess or sweat or tears involved.

Transformation—whether we're talking about a house or a heart—is not a pretty process. True rehabilitation, true change only happens when the old, crumbling, moldy, and rusty parts are stripped away, revealing the naked truth underneath. It's only when we are elbow-deep in mud and muck that we can see the strong, shining bones below on which we can build something beautiful.

Even during seasons of reflection and repentance, we can be tempted to put too much emphasis on the "after" part of a transformation. Sure, everyone loves gasping and applauding at the big reveal at the end of a home improvement show. And it is absolutely inspiring to read about someone's triumph over adversity, especially when the hero used to be an underdog.

But what about when that excavation and rehabilitation takes place in our hearts and our lives? When we are only willing to direct our gaze on the after pictures, we're missing the hard-fought beauty of that behind-the-scenes battle. We're missing out on the chance to more fully understand the sacrifice that led to the victory, to more completely appreciate the reward that only came as a result of the work. And we're missing the whole truth about who we are and how vast the gap between "before" and "after" truly is.

It took me a while, but I realize now that the day my neighbor's house was at its ugliest and messiest was actually the most amazing one of its entire transformation. Because without that day, I couldn't possibly appreciate its new siding and shutters and landscaping and front porch light. Unless I face the destruction, I can't understand the magnitude of the recreation.

This truth is no different when it comes to our journey to the cross during this Lent season. If I wait until I've "got it all together" to reveal my struggles, I'm robbing God of the opportunity to shine through my ugliness and my mess. I'm forgetting that He is the only one who can make me a new creation, and He won't transform me until I lay myself bare before Him and let Him get to work.

When my house is falling apart, that is the time to open up to God and to others. Not later. Not when I get it figured out. Not when I've painted and polished and perfected it all. If I waited for that day, I'd never have a story to tell, for we are all in constant change, constant sharpening and growing and transforming. So when our houses are falling apart, that is the day we should look up, accept the Lord's help, and meet our neighbor's eyes. Doing this will undoubtedly help us be more patient, more gentle—with each other and with ourselves. And as we turn to the cross and the One who loves us at our ugliest and promises to redeem our worst messes, it will certainly reveal to us the true beauty of transformation.

Dear God, Forgive me. Forgive me for judging other people's messes and hiding my own. Forgive me for believing I can fix my problems and make over my life by myself. I know that's not true, but I'm no longer discouraged by that fact because I know You can redeem all things. Thank You, God. Thank You for loving me at my ugliest and messiest. Thank You for never turning away when I am falling apart. And thank You for creating in me a clean heart and restoring my spirit. Please help me remember that You are the builder and the artist my house and my heart need. I love You, Lord. Amen.

QUESTIONS TO CONSIDER

1. Are you going through the in-between part of transformation right now? Or are you ashamed by the messy, ugly parts of your life right now? In what ways do you need to lay yourself bare before God, and ask Him to get to work?

_____

_____

_____

_____

2. Have you turned to God to help you restore what has been broken? Have you asked Him to redeem the situation that you're facing? Why or why not?

_____

_____

_____

_____

3. Who can you let in to walk with you through this process?

_____

_____

_____

_____

DAY 8
REFLECTION

As you grow closer to God during this time, meditate on not just what He's done for you but also who He is. Reflect on these characteristics of God.

INFINITE AND ETERNAL

"I am the Alpha and the Omega," says the Lord God, "the one who is, who was, and who is to come, the Almighty."

REVELATION 1:8

OMNIPOTENT (ALL-POWERFUL)

Jesus looked at them and said, "With man this is impossible, but with God all things are possible."

MATTHEW 19:26

OMNISCIENT (ALL-KNOWING)

Lord, you have searched me and known me.
You know when I sit down and when I stand up;
you understand my thoughts from far away.
You observe my travels and my rest;
you are aware of all my ways.
Before a word is on my tongue,
you know all about it, Lord.

PSALM 139:1–4

MERCIFUL

But God, who is rich in mercy, because of his great love that
he had for us, made us alive with Christ even though we were
dead in trespasses. You are saved by grace!

EPHESIANS 2:4-5

JUST

Turn away from evil, do what is good, and settle permanently.
For the LORD loves justice and will not abandon his
faithful ones.

They are kept safe forever, but the children of the wicked will
be destroyed. The righteous will inherit the land and dwell in
it permanently.

PSALM 37:27-29

LOVING

Dear friends, let us love one another, because love is from
God, and everyone who loves has been born of God and
knows God. The one who does not love does not know God,
because God is love.

1 JOHN 4:7-8

Which attributes do you find easiest to connect with and express thanksgiving for? Which are the most difficult for you?

Unconditional

Lord, you showed favor to your land; you restored the fortunes of Jacob.

You forgave your people's guilt; you covered all their sin. Selah

You withdrew all your fury; you turned from your burning anger.

Return to us, God of our salvation, and abandon your displeasure with us.

Will you be angry with us forever? Will you prolong your anger for all generations?

Will you not revive us again so that your people may rejoice in you?

Show us your faithful love, Lord, and give us your salvation.

PSALM 85:1–7

"How many times have I told you?"

"Why should I believe you when you've said the same thing before?"

"Don't you remember how nice I was to you today? And then you do this?"

"I'm done! I mean it. This is it. I can't take anymore."

I've said these words. I've said them so many times I couldn't begin to keep track of their frequency, much less their effectiveness. For all their use, you might assume they must do the job. Those searing sentences must cut their recipients to the quick, poking them right in the conscience, right in the deepest part of their hearts. Clearly my word-arrows strike their targets and initiate repentance and change.

Right? Not so much.

Over the past few years, I've realized that I am guilty of loving conditionally. As my daughters have grown older and my marriage has grown stronger, I've been forced to face some of the challenges I bring to my most dear relationships—and one of the biggest is the ball of strings I have tied to my love.

Perhaps you've struggled with this, too. Maybe you also want every advantage of God's unconditional love but are reluctant to offer that same gift to others. That realization stings, doesn't it?

Looking in the mirror is hard, friend. It's hard when our jeans are tight or our face is broken out, and it's hard when our sin nature is slipping through the cracks. It's hard when we see the expectations we place on people we call beloved, when we see the score sheet we keep against the very people on our team, and it's hard when we realize how far short our love falls from the love our Father gives us so freely.

God will forgive us every time, and no matter what, He will LOVE us with an unfailing love. No Strings attached.

In Psalm 85 the author is begging God for forgiveness, for another chance, for one more redemption story. He's remembering all the times God has forgiven His people completely, and he's believing that God will do it once again. And He will. He promises that.

Our God is faithful, just as the psalmist says. He will forgive us every time because all our sins have already been paid for by Jesus. No more debt to pay. And no matter what, He will love us with an unfailing love. No strings attached.

As we journey to the cross together, I am overwhelmingly thankful for God's faithful love and the example He gives us in loving unconditionally. When I read through the Old Testament and into the Psalms, I can't help shake my head at the Israelites. Those fickle, faithless Israelites . . . who . . . just might have more in common with me than I want to admit. Yet, because of Christ, God never shakes His head at me. He never shouts in exasperation, "How many times have I told you?" and He never, ever says, "I'm done." Let us thank God for His faithful love—and ask Him to teach us to love faithfully too.

Dear God, thank You for loving so much better than I do. Thank You for being faithful to offer me grace and forgiveness, to love me unconditionally even when I don't deserve it. Please help me love others the same way, Lord. Help me be slow to anger and quick to forgive. Help me see with Your eyes and love with Your love, no strings attached. Thank You, God. I love You. Amen.

QUESTIONS TO CONSIDER

1. Do you have a hard time loving others as unconditionally as the Lord loves us?

_____

_____

_____

_____

_____

_____

2. Is it possible you also put conditions on your love for God as well?

_____

_____

_____

_____

_____

_____

3. If you need to apologize to anyone for loving them with strings attached, can you find time to do that this week? Make a note for this in your schedule.

_____

_____

_____

_____

_____

_____

_____

_____

_____

_____

_____

_____

_____

_____

_____

_____

_____

_____

_____

DAY 10
PRAYER

Dear Holy and Wonderful God,

You are amazing. You are awesome, and I am in awe! I'm overwhelmed by the thought that You would be mindful of me, that You would consider me friend and call me daughter, that You would love me.

Thank You, Lord. You are mighty and powerful, perfect and holy, merciful and just, and You show me this in the face of Christ, who journeyed toward me so that I may know You. I worship You for such a gift. I give You all the praise and honor and glory; I give You everything I have in me and everything I am. I long to see You—face-to-face for eternity, but also in the everyday here on earth. Reveal Yourself to me, Lord. Draw me near and hold me close. Never let me go.

As I march toward the cross this spring, God, I pray that I would encounter You in a meaningful way. I pray that I would be changed. I pray that Your will be done. Thank You, God. I love You. Amen.

Fasting

"Whenever you fast, don't be gloomy like the hypocrites. For they make their faces unattractive so that their fasting is obvious to people. Truly I tell you, they have their reward. But when you fast, put oil on your head and wash your face, so that your fasting isn't obvious to others but to your Father who is in secret. And your Father who sees in secret will reward you."

MATTHEW 6:16–18

Though I grew up going to church, I never really heard about fasting until I went to college. My introduction to the practice was rudimentary, but when Lent rolled around my freshman year, I thought I understood enough to take part. After all, it's what my friends were doing to prepare for Easter, so I figured it would be good for me too.

Determined to grow in my faith (or at least look as holy as my friends), I committed to giving up soda. Though this was obviously nowhere close to the level of sacrifice Jesus has offered for me, I was new to the idea and wanted to begin with a baby step. For my first attempt at fasting, I chose something that I liked but wasn't dependent on. I was setting myself up for success, if you will.

Going without soda was pretty easy. I didn't actually drink a lot of it, so it was just about the slowest on-ramp to fasting I could have chosen. I went back to water in the dorm's cafeteria and informed my roommate of my deep commitment to fasting every time she pulled a can out of our mini-fridge. I was definitely getting an A in How to be a Christian College Student 101.

Until I went home one weekend, that is.

My family didn't drink a lot of soda, but we always had root beer with pizza and Mexican food. It's just what we did. That habit was so ingrained in me that when I sat down to a big burrito and glass of cold root beer at my parents' table, I didn't think a thing of it.

I mindlessly ate that burrito and washed it down with my drink until it hit me. Cup to lips, hand frozen, eyes large, I realized I had been drinking soda. We drink root beer with burritos, and root beer is soda! I'd forgotten my commitment to fast. I'd broken my promise to myself and to God. I'd failed at what I thought was the easiest first fasting plan I could make.

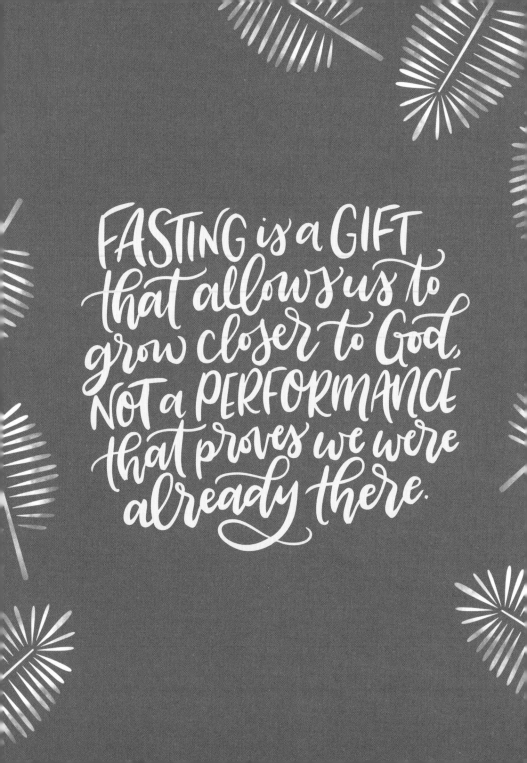

FASTING is a GIFT
that allows us to
grow closer to God,
NOT a PERFORMANCE
that proves we were
already there.

As an all-or-nothing perfectionist (especially one who had a whole lot of head knowledge about grace but still believed she needed to earn God's favor, at least just a little bit), I was devastated. Jesus gave up His life for me, and I couldn't even give up a few ounces of root beer! I made it to Easter that year without drinking any more soda, but rather than use the fast to draw nearer to God, I simply felt like a failure, so unworthy of salvation that I couldn't even really celebrate the fact that He gave His life anyway.

The next year my fasting experience was even worse. Determined to not only avoid breaking my fast mindlessly, but also to give up much more than a measly beverage, I decided I would fast from all food one day a week.

Long story short, it didn't go well. I was starving and miserable—and I made sure everyone around me knew it. I didn't literally walk around wailing and gnashing my teeth, but I might as well have. I was the picture of a hypocrite, just as Jesus described in Matthew 6—gloomy and grouchy and making much of myself.

That fast ended well before Easter because, thankfully, I realized my heart was far from right. I was practicing a discipline simply for show, longing to prove to my friends, to God, and to myself that I was a Very Good Christian. I didn't fast in response to Jesus' sacrifice. I didn't do it to remove distractions so I could focus on God. And I didn't remove something in order to add more Jesus to my life, that's for sure.

Personal fasting is meant to be a private practice, an act of obedience that we keep between ourselves and our Lord. It's meant to refine us, not to impress others. It's a gift that allows us to grow closer to God, not a performance that proves we were already there.

Are you fasting this Lent season? Are you making room for Jesus in your life and your heart? Are you seeking clarity as you commune with the Lord, asking Him to cleanse your mind and heart so you can more fully appreciate and celebrate the resurrection? If you are, I pray you do it from a place of honor and humility. I pray it brings you closer to Jesus, as He sees what you do in secret this season.

Dear God, thank You for giving me this space, this season of Lent, to draw close to You and ready my heart for Easter. I don't want Easter to be just another holiday, simply a day for family, dressing up, eating a big meal, and hunting for eggs. I want it to truly be a celebration of the enormous sacrifice You made when You gave Your life for mine. I want to worship You and thank You and appreciate You more than ever before, and I know this time of preparation will help me do that. Please guide me in the disciplines I choose so I can make much of You and less of me. Please help me remove distractions, honor the gift of salvation, and allow You to cleanse me of any sin between us. Thank You, Lord, for loving me enough to refine me, to save me, to draw me near. I love You. Amen.

QUESTIONS TO CONSIDER

1. Have you ever tried fasting? What was your experience like?

_____

_____

_____

_____

_____

2. If you've never tried fasting, would you consider it during this season of Lent? If not, what's holding you back?

_____

_____

_____

_____

_____

3. If you don't understand fasting, where or from whom could you learn more?

_____

_____

_____

_____

DAY 12
REFLECTION

The first commandment forbids believers from having any other god beside the Almighty God (Exodus 20:3).

When you look at your life and your habits, do you see any gods?

_____

_____

_____

_____

Where are you spending your time, your energy, your resources, your attention, and your affection?

_____

_____

_____

_____

_____

_____

Sometimes too much of a good thing can become an idol. Have you made gods out of anything the Lord has given you?

_____

_____

_____

_____

_____

Is it possible God may be asking you to give up something that's stealing your focus from Him, whether that means forever or for just a season?

_____

_____

_____

_____

_____

_____

_____

_____

_____

Jesus called them over and said to them, "You know that those who are regarded as rulers of the Gentiles lord it over them, and those in high positions act as tyrants over them. But it is not so among you. On the contrary, whoever wants to become great among you will be your servant, and whoever wants to be first among you will be a slave to all. For even the Son of Man did not come to be served, but to serve, and to give his life as a ransom for many."

MARK 10:42–45

"Go on! Go up there! Don't let her take your credit!"

My co-worker and friend was trying to help, literally pushing me toward the stage as our manager accepted applause for the event I had just planned and pulled off. She had watched my face fall and my eyes fill with tears as I watched someone else honored for the hard work I'd put in for the past several months, and she knew it wasn't fair. Since my heart had sunk to the floor and my feet had turned into lead, I couldn't take a step on my own. So that friend ended up pulling me through the crowd and shoving me up to center stage. Little did she know that the battle I was fighting in that moment was with myself, not my manager.

It was my first real job after college, a non-profit I was incredibly passionate about, and I was desperate to prove myself successful. I craved attention and credit—so much so that I eventually lost focus of the charitable reasons for the organization's work. I'd taken the job because I wanted to help people, but I'd gotten caught up in office politics and my own pride, and I'd become more concerned with making a name for myself than making a difference in people's lives.

Shortly after that incident, I left that job—and went on to several other jobs where I started out wanting to help people, but eventually found myself struggling with pride and resentment over my status (or lack thereof). At the time I wondered why I couldn't find the right job, but in hindsight I now realize God was patiently refining my motives and priorities as I slowly learned how to put others first and truly serve them.

One of my favorite things about the Gospels is the way we get to see the disciples interact with Jesus. If we get enough distance from actual Scripture and forget the details of the stories in Matthew, Mark, Luke, and John, we might begin putting the disciples on pedestals, imagining them to be superstar believers with all the answers and an inside track to our Lord. If we aren't careful, we can sometimes forget how human they really were.

The truth is, they were just a bunch of guys who sometimes got it right, but more often than not, stumbled their way through life with Jesus. They often forgot what they'd just learned or heard, proving that they didn't really listen in the first place. In this passage of Mark, two of the disciples had the audacity to ask Jesus to promise them prime seating in heaven. The other disciples didn't like that one bit, and the group of followers began to argue. Jesus quickly put a stop to that by telling them that whoever wants to be first will actually be last and the one willing to be last will be put first.

What a paradigm shift for the disciples! What a shift for us! We may not all spend our early careers letting our pride get the best of us (like me) or essentially try calling shotgun in Jesus' car (like the disciples). But we all possess the human nature that inherently desires honor and praise. In some way or another, we all struggle with making ourselves little gods, forgetting to love either God or our neighbors.

For me—maybe for you too?—pride is forever something I will have to fight, placing it at Jesus' feet over and over again. As I forget the lessons He's taught me and slip back into the habit of striving for first place, I have to consistently repent for hustling to earn credit and attention and success. Choosing humility is a year-round, life-long battle. But in these weeks leading to the cross, where the most perfect, blameless, holy Man lowered Himself to take not the credit but all the blame for us, we can really lean into the invitation Jesus gives us to humble ourselves and seek Him.

Lent is a time when we should really lean into the invitation Jesus gives us to HUMBLE ourselves and SEEK HIM.

Do you struggle with pride? Is it hard to live out the idea of the first being last and the last being first? Do you find it hard to comprehend true servant leadership, the kind Jesus modeled—and asks of us? You are not alone—and we are not defenseless in this fight. The Bible tells us in 1 John 1:9 that "If we confess our sins, he is faithful and righteous to forgive us our sins and to cleanse us from all unrighteousness."

If we pray and seek His face, if we humble ourselves, confess, and turn from our sin—the very thing we are spending these forty days of Lent doing—He will forgive us. And that is something worth praise and applause!

Oh Lord, I'm so sorry. I'm sorry I let my pride get out of control again and put myself first again. I'm sorry I made my own needs priority over the needs of others. I'm sorry I forgot Who truly reigns. You are God, and I am not. You are almighty and worthy of all my praise! Thank You for guiding me back to You every time I get turned around. Thank You for reminding me, just like You reminded the disciples, that the only One worthy of worship is the One who humbled Himself to the point of death, for me. I love You, Lord, and I'm so grateful for this time to focus on You, not me. Amen.

QUESTIONS TO CONSIDER

1. Have you ever found yourself desperate for attention or credit for your hard work?

2. What does it mean to you that the first shall be last and the last shall be first?

3. What is one practical way you can make more of Jesus and less of yourself today?

DAY 14
PSALM 103

My soul, bless the LORD, and all that is within me,
  bless his holy name.
My soul, bless the LORD, and do not forget all
  his benefits.

He forgives all your iniquity; he heals all
  your diseases.
He redeems your life from the Pit; he crowns you
  with faithful love and compassion.
He satisfies you with good things; your youth is
  renewed like the eagle.

The LORD executes acts of righteousness and justice
  for all the oppressed.
He revealed his ways to Moses, his deeds to the
  people of Israel.
The LORD is compassionate and gracious, slow to
  anger and abounding in faithful love.
He will not always accuse us or be angry forever.
He has not dealt with us as our sins deserve or
  repaid us according to our iniquities.

For as high as the heavens are above the earth,
    so great is his faithful love toward those
    who fear him.
As far as the east is from the west, so far has he
    removed our transgressions from us.
As a father has compassion on his children, so the
    Lord has compassion on those who fear him.
For he knows what we are made of, remembering
    that we are dust.

As for man, his days are like grass—he blooms like
    a flower of the field;
when the wind passes over it, it vanishes, and its
    place is no longer known.
But from eternity to eternity the Lord's faithful love
    is toward those who fear him,
and his righteousness toward the grandchildren
of those who keep his covenant, who remember to
    observe his precepts.
The Lord has established his throne in heaven, and
    his kingdom rules over all.

Bless the Lord, all his angels of great strength, who
    do his word, obedient to his command.
Bless the Lord, all his armies, his servants who
    do his will.
Bless the Lord, all his works in all the places where
    he rules. My soul, bless the Lord!

Fasting as Service

"Why have we fasted, but you have not seen? We have denied ourselves, but you haven't noticed!"

"Look, you do as you please on the day of your fast, and oppress all your workers. You fast with contention and strife to strike viciously with your fist. You cannot fast as you do today, hoping to make your voice heard on high.

Will the fast I choose be like this: A day for a person to deny himself, to bow his head like a reed, and to spread out sackcloth and ashes? Will you call this a fast and a day acceptable to the LORD?

Isn't this the fast I choose: To break the chains of wickedness, to untie the ropes of the yoke, to set the oppressed free, and to tear off every yoke? Is it not to share your bread with the hungry, to bring the poor and homeless into your house, to clothe the naked when you see him, and not to ignore your own flesh and blood?

Then your light will appear like the dawn, and your recovery will come quickly. Your righteousness will go before you, and the LORD's glory will be your rear guard.

At that time, when you call, the LORD will answer; when you cry out, he will say, 'Here I am.' If you get rid of the yoke among you, the finger-pointing and malicious speaking, and if you offer yourself to the hungry, and satisfy the afflicted one, then your light will shine in the darkness, and your night will be like noonday.

The LORD will always lead you, satisfy you in a parched land, and strengthen your bones. You will be like a watered garden and like a spring whose water never runs dry.

ISAIAH 58:3–11

More times than I'd like to admit, the Easter season sneaks up on me. The first couple months of the year are always a tug of war between my goal-setting, plan-obsessed perfectionism and the gray fog of sadness that seems to descend each year when snow, sickness, and my own self derail many of those plans I made. So by the time I begin seeing signs of spring, I'm often just barely holding on. Somehow, I find myself surprised, once again, to feel the weather warming up just a touch and hear people announce what they are sacrificing for Lent.

This year, though, I was determined to be more intentional. I've been studying the discipline of Lent, after all, and am more convinced than ever of the importance of taking this time to reflect on God, to repent and sacrifice, to endure temptation and focus on the Lord, and to prepare for the coming celebration of the resurrection. I wasn't sure, though, if that meant I had to "give something up" for Lent.

I considered some sort of social media or technology fast. After all, I certainly spend way more time online and glued to a screen than I should. It would be a true sacrifice to give up both the tools and the entertainment those things offer, and it would free up time to spend focused on the Lord. And, the less-than-pure-hearted part of my mind whispered, Brilliant! You've been wanting to declutter and streamline your digital world anyway. A win-win arrangement.

Win-win? As I debated fasting during Lent, I was once again looking for a way to do it that would benefit me. I was looking for a way that was convenient, a choice that would help me reach my personal goals while also, hopefully, scoring some points with God. Will I never learn?!

The book of Isaiah tells the story of God's people, of their judgment and their restoration. It has historical context but also present-day relevance. Every single time I read about the Israelites and their struggle to stay faithful, I want to shout out loud, "Will you never learn?!" And every single time I start feeling superior to God's people, He reminds me that I'm one of them. Just like the Israelites, I make the same mistakes over and over again. Just like His people, I am restored and redeemed, only to turn back to the sin that led me to the wilderness last time. Just like them, it sometimes feels like I will never learn.

Can you relate? Do you struggle with the same sin, over and over again? Do you find yourself in need of God's mercy and redemption repeatedly? Do you forget what God has done for you—so easily, so quickly?

You are not alone. And thankfully, God is exceedingly patient and loving, and though He may allow us to suffer the consequences of our choices, He never leaves us alone. And He always rescues us, restores us, redeems us.

In chapter 58 of Isaiah, the Israelites express frustration that they've fasted just like they're supposed to, but God isn't fixing their hard situation. God's reply is to point out their hypocrisy and the emptiness of their gesture. He isn't impressed or blessed by their sacrifice, because He knows it's only for show. He knows they're only doing it to get something in return. So, once again, He explains what true sacrifice is.

True sacrifice isn't merely denying yourself until you feel (and look) miserable. It's giving of yourself to help others. It's feeding the hungry and freeing the oppressed. It's tending to God's children instead of protecting your own interests.

On the same day I was considering a social media fast (and also longing for a spring cleaning of my online life), I received an invitation to join a Facebook group. It came from a friend at church for a group designed to communicate needs of foster children in our community. And my initial, gut-level honest reaction was dismay.

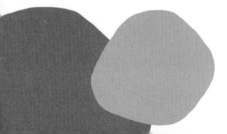

Join another Facebook group?

But I already get the emails!

This is just going to add to the noise . . .

But how will it look if I don't accept the invite?

Just like the Israelites, I was once again focused on myself and what I could get out of every interaction. But just like He did for the Israelites, God didn't let me stay in that pit of pride and hypocrisy long. As quickly as I had those traitorous thoughts, I remembered my commitment to observe Lent the way it was designed: with intention and humility and sacrifice. I clicked "accept invitation" and gave thanks to God for the opportunity to try again.

If you've chosen to fast during this Lent season, consider how that sacrifice can be used not only as a thankful response to what Jesus did on the cross, but as a missional picture of the cross to others, laying down your life so that others can see the God who did the same for them. In other words, consider how you could also use this time to be the hands and feet of God, how you could intentionally seek opportunities to serve others, to share your bread and shine your light. Then, God promises, He will satisfy you and strengthen you. Then He will accept your sacrifice and make you like a spring that never runs dry.

Heavenly Father, Holy God, thank You for Your patience. Thank You for Your guidance. Thank You for loving me enough to redirect my steps every time I stumble and get lost. Thank You for loving me enough to stay with me, to rescue me, to redeem every single situation. I love You, Lord, and I'm so grateful for everything You've given me, everything You've done. I want to give You everything in return. I want to give You something of value. I want to do what You've asked and help others instead of helping myself. Please show me how. Give me opportunities to feed the hungry and free the oppressed. Compel me to reach out, to offer help, to love my neighbor so they, too, can know how much You love them. In my sacrifice during this season, help me reveal Jesus, who sacrificed everything to save us all. Forgive me for every time I've gotten this wrong. Accept my sacrifice of love, of gratitude, of worship. Amen.

QUESTIONS TO CONSIDER

1. Are you tempted to look for win-win solutions when considering how to respond to God? What do you think you are really after when you approach God this way? What are you looking for?

_____

_____

_____

_____

2. Think about how you are serving or responding to God in this season. Are your choices all about Him—or all about you? Why?

_____

_____

_____

_____

3. During this season of Lent, how can you sacrifice not just in response to Jesus but also in service to His people?

_____

_____

_____

_____

DAY 16
GRATITUDE JOURNALING

"When I give thanks . . . I make a place for God to grow within me."

—ALICE WALKER

Gratitude is a sacrifice—of self and pride, of significance and reputation. It requires us to become vulnerable, to humble ourselves, to courageously present our thanksgiving as offering.

What do you need to give up or let go of in order to offer open hands—of worship, of sacrifice, of gratitude—to God?

_____

_____

_____

_____

_____

_____

As you allow Him to strip away the unnecessary and the unholy, what blessings are you beginning to grasp? What are you grateful for today?

_____

_____

_____

_____

_____

_____

Giving Up Lies

We know how much God loves us, and we have put our trust in his love.

1 JOHN 4:16A NLT

A few years ago, I went through a rough season in the friendship arena. I felt rejected, disappointed, deserted, and excluded. I was certain that nobody liked me, nobody cared, and if I were a couple decades younger I just might have finished that little rant with, "I guess I'll just eat worms."

And speaking of younger days, I definitely experienced a few flashbacks to my middle school years in that time. You know the ones—when I desperately wanted the cool kids to like me but it never seemed to work out that way. They didn't notice me or when they did, they didn't like what they saw. And that's just how I felt going through that time when friends seemed few and far between.

I don't know about you, but I find it way too easy to move from thinking sad thoughts about the situation to thinking sad thoughts about myself when I'm faced with rejection. Feeling hurt and alone, I quickly begin believing things like . . .

If I were cooler, they'd like me.

If I shopped here or worked out there, they'd invite me to the party.

If I wasn't such a dork, they'd want to hang out with me.

If I were thinner . . .

If I didn't make so many stupid jokes . . .

If I had more time or more money . . .

If I weren't so me . . .

To be clear—these are actual thoughts I've had as an adult. I'm not reminiscing about the awkward years of adolescence. Nope. I've actually let those words enter my grown-up brain. Thankfully, I'm decades past letting those thoughts get too comfortable in my mind or my heart. They might make their way in, but it's not like I'm throwing open the door and offering them a warm beverage and my favorite spot on the couch.

Thankfully, I've learned over the years to call these thoughts what they are—lies—and I've learned that the only way to combat their attack is with a hefty dose of truth. And what better time to give up believing the enemy's lies about who we are than right now, as we approach the resurrection?

As we take time to intentionally pursue a deeper understanding of and relationship with God, we must allow Him to strip us of everything that comes between us. And that includes lies we've been believing about our worth and our purpose, about our past and our future. Whenever insecurity strikes and lies sneak into our thoughts—whether because of difficult relationships or some other circumstance—we must recognize them as false and then replace them with truth.

For example, when I think about the time I ordered eight pizzas on the first night of a small group I was leading and nobody showed up, I could so easily spiral into a pit of dejection and bitterness. But instead, I remind myself of the times I've had so many friends at my house that we ran out of chairs and ended up using coolers and piano benches for seating.

And when I begin thinking that a rejection or disappointment is a result of my inability to measure up (I'm not smart enough, fun enough, creative enough, organized enough, thin enough, outgoing enough), I open up God's Word for a dose of reality and a reminder of who—and Whose—I am.

While we're taking time to eliminate the things that distract us from drawing close to the Lord during this season, let's get rid of the lies this world has told us, leaving room for the truth of God's Word. If we give up lies for Lent, we just might find we're filled with a better understanding of who God is and who He says we are. These verses have helped me remember just what God says is true about me:

Now this is what the LORD says—
the one who created you, Jacob,
and the one who formed you, Israel—

"Do not fear, for I have redeemed you;
I have called you by your name; you are mine.

I will be with you
when you pass through the waters,
and when you pass through the rivers,
they will not overwhelm you.

You will not be scorched
when you walk through the fire,
and the flame will not burn you.

For I am the LORD your God,
the Holy One of Israel, and your Savior.

I have given Egypt as a ransom for you,
Cush and Seba in your place.

Because you are precious in my sight
and honored, and I love you,

I will give people in exchange for you
and nations instead of your life.

ISAIAH 43:1–4 (MSG)

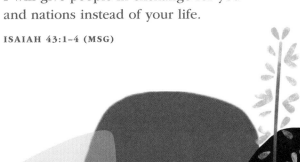

See that? We are His. We are loved. The mighty God of this universe would do anything for us—*and He has by dying on the cross for our sin and overcoming death by rising again.* I love the way *The Message* ends that passage: "That's how much you mean to me! That's how much I love you! I'd sell off the whole world to get you back, trade the creation just for you."

Amen, and let's not forget it again! Let's not dwell in the lies any longer. Let's get rid of every single half-truth and blatant lie, every hint of fear and doubt and insecurity—and then let's watch as God fills us up with the beautiful truth of His love.

Dear God, I need Your help. I'm so confused and twisted up, caught up in the doubts and insecurities that I can't seem to get out of my head! I know what You say about me, but it doesn't feel true. Can You help? Will You help me get rid of anything that is not true? I want to give up lies for Lent—and for good. I want to stay focused on You and what You say is right and true and good. Please help me, Lord. Show me the truth and help me resist the temptation to believe anything else. Open my eyes to what You want me to hear and protect me from the fear and rejection and disappointment that will surely lead me further from You rather than closer. Help me draw near, God. Take away the lies standing between us. Forgive me for letting my eyes and my heart stray from You. Thank You for reminding me what's true. I love You, Lord. Amen.

QUESTIONS TO CONSIDER

1. Can you think of a time you experienced rejection or disappointment? How did that affect what you believed to be true about yourself, about the world, or about God?

_____

_____

_____

_____

2. What lies are you believing today? What do you need to do in order to give them up—for Lent and for good? Be specific.

_____

_____

_____

_____

3. Is there someone in your life who might need to hear the truth today? How can you encourage him or her to let go of hurtful lies and turn back to healing truth?

_____

_____

_____

_____

DAY 18
REFLECTION

In *Mere Christianity,* C. S. Lewis wrote, "A proud man is always looking down on things and people; and, of course, as long as you are looking down, you cannot see something that is above you." Do you struggle with pride? Are your eyes so focused on the credit others owe you that you've lost sight of God?

When do you find yourself overly concerned with credit or reputation?

When is it hardest for you to put the needs of others before your own?

In what ways did Jesus humble Himself for you?

How can you intentionally put others first during this season of Lent?

_____

_____

_____

Who in your life can you give credit to, minister to, or encourage?

_____

_____

_____

What do you think could change in your relationship with God if you humbled yourself and repented from the sin of pride?

_____

_____

_____

_____

_____

_____

_____

Exposed

My brothers and sisters, if any among you strays from the truth, and someone turns him back, let that person know that whoever turns a sinner from the error of his way will save his soul from death and cover a multitude of sins.

JAMES 5:19–20

I'm sitting at Panera on a Sunday afternoon. I got here early enough to snag a booth for my laptop and me, but as the lunch crowd has grown I've grown self-conscious. *People are probably mad that I'm taking up a whole booth,* I think. *I should get up and move.* But as I crane my neck to look for a smaller table, preferably one near an outlet, I only see people settling into chairs or carrying trays of sandwiches and salads.

No problem. I'll just get up to refill my cup, and while I'm walking to the drink station, I'll look for a table.

So I do. I slide out of my booth, refill my cup with iced tea, eyes darting around the restaurant to locate a seat that won't impose on other customers quite as much. I don't see anything, so I go back to my booth, slide in, and start to stick my earbuds back in my ears. That's when she tapped me on the shoulder.

I looked up into the smiling face of an older woman who said, gently, "I'd want someone to tell me . . . so . . ."

She then kindly informed me that the back of my skirt—an overly long, full affair that had been annoying me all day long—was caught in my waistband. As she saw the horror appear in my eyes, she reassured me that nobody had seen a thing because (thankfully) I was wearing a slip. We chuckled about how my mom raised me right (right = wearing a slip under skirts, obviously), and I thanked her profusely. She walked back to her table, and I sat at mine, no longer worried about offending customers by taking up a table meant for four.

Clearly, I had bigger, more humiliating offenses to worry about!

The coincidence—or, more accurately, the painfully tangible confirmation of something God has recently taught me—makes me chuckle. At the very moment I learned about my exposed backside, I was working on a writing project, one that relies on Scripture more than anything I've ever written. Just a few weeks before, I'd messaged my manager, double checking that an editor would carefully review my work before it reaches the public. I've grown up in the church and know Scripture fairly well, but a biblical scholar I am not. Not even close! And the thought of making a mistake with the Word of God and of that mistake being left uncovered or un-fixed for all the world to see was enough to bring on small bursts of panic (and not a small amount of writer's block!). My manager assured me that editors and experts would check my work; they wouldn't publish any heresy with my name on it.

It wasn't long ago that asking for an editor would be the last thing this perfectionistic and prideful writer would have done. After all, I'm not just a writer; I'm also an editor. What could anyone possibly teach me?!

Yikes. I know. That line of thought is ugly, but it's real. Thankfully, though, it's growing faint as God teaches me to be teachable, as He's showing me to hold my words and my knowledge and even my convictions loosely in light of His Truth. It's not been easy; peeling off layers of pride never is. But it's been good. It's been good to recognize my sin and feel God's prompting to let it go and to grow into someone who may not know everything but truly knows the One who does.

When the woman at Panera pointed out my exposed backside, I was mortified. I could feel my face burn bright pink as she patted my shoulder, and I couldn't decide if her kindness made the whole situation better or worse. When she left me alone, I sat staring at my laptop screen. *What do I do now?* I wondered. I could have buried my head, I could have gathered my misbehaving skirt and left, I could

have texted my friend who convinced me to buy the skirt and inform her that my humiliation was all her fault.

Instead of all that I chose to covertly yank my skirt back into respectability and move across the aisle to the table with the outlet for my low-battery laptop. I wouldn't say I held my head high, but I did think for a while about how many people saw me and didn't say anything, about how one woman braved an uncomfortable conversation with a stranger and did.

As she finished her lunch and left, she stopped by my new table. I pulled out an earbud and looked up. She smiled and said, "Remember our deal." I smiled politely and nodded, not sure what she meant at first. But then I realized she meant that we'd made a deal to tell someone when her slip is showing. And then I smiled for real.

Though embarrassing, a twisted skirt, a tag on the outside, or a typo are easy gaffes to point out or to have pointed out to us. But sometimes we need our sisters to gently tell us we've made larger mistakes. When a friend keeps making excuses for her harmful choices, we need to be brave enough to talk to her about it. And when a friend approaches us about our recent slide back into old habits, ones we vowed to never pick up again, we have a choice. We can react with anger or run and hide, or we can thank her for having the courage to say something.

Sometimes we need to be guided or reminded; we need to be taught the truth or pulled back to what we knew deep down. And sometimes we need to be the brave one to tell someone else. It's easy to notice and look away, to snicker or point, to assume it's not your problem or your business. It's much harder to gently let someone know her slip is showing.

But as my new friend in Panera reminded me, "I'd want someone to tell me." And like I told her (and repeated to myself), I'm so glad she did.

Mention of fasting typically makes us think of food, technology, or other consumable things we might give up for a season. But what if God is asking for a different type of fast? What if He's calling us to turn away from certain sins (like pride) or tendencies (like avoiding hard topics)?

What would happen if we chose to sacrifice our comfort as we lean into this deeper relationship with Christ?

I may have consumed plenty of carbs and coffee that day, but I walked away lighter after choosing to lay down my pride and learn from the lesson God was teaching me with an unruly skirt and a kind neighbor. As you continue your journey to the cross, I pray you can lay down your own bad habits in order to fully experience the growth that comes only through uninhibited communion with the Lord.

Dear God, thank You for the friends old and new who are brave enough to hold me accountable. Thank You for the conviction You place on my heart when I remain blind to my sin and the damage my choices might create. Thank You for showing me how much better it is to admit my mistakes, to ask for forgiveness, and to grow into the person you created me to be. Lord, I ask that You search my heart and show me any place where I'm following myself instead of following You. And please help me accept Your correction, feeling grateful not offended. Thank You, God. Thank You for loving me just as I am but desiring so much more for me. Thank You for refusing to leave me alone in my sin and for constantly pulling me back to you. I love you, Lord. Amen.

QUESTIONS TO CONSIDER

1. Has a friend (or stranger) ever brought a mistake or bad choice to your attention? How did you receive their correction?

2. Have you ever been brave enough to tell someone else about a sin or habit you've witnessed in their life? How did that person react?

3. Are you willing to ask God to expose any sin in your life right now? Why or why not?

DAY 20
PRAYER

Merciful and loving Father,

I come to You broken, open, and laid bare. You have searched me and stripped away everything that's kept me from You, and I'm grateful. You have shown me my sin and reminded me of Your sacrifice for it, and I give You all my thanks. I don't want to be proud, Lord; banish any remaining pride from my heart.

This is holy ground that You've allowed me to touch, God, and I don't want to leave. I want to abide in You, to remain in Your presence, to turn away from anything that might come between us. Please keep me humble, Lord. Keep me watchful for the ways the world tries to distract me, and keep my eyes open for opportunities of service so I can display who You are to others. Protect my heart; remind me every day that You are God and I am not.

I don't want to leave this season of Lent unchanged, Lord. I don't want to return to my proud ways, my distracted days. I want to stay right here with You, with not one thing pulling me from You. Please help me stay in this posture, this mind-set, this holy communion with You forever.

In Jesus' name I pray,

Amen.

DAY 21

True Confession

Even now—
this is the LORD's declaration—
turn to me with all your heart,
with fasting, weeping, and mourning.
Tear your hearts,
not just your clothes,
and return to the LORD your God.
For he is gracious and compassionate,
slow to anger, abounding in faithful love,
and he relents from sending disaster.
Who knows? He may turn and relent
and leave a blessing behind him,
so you can offer grain and wine
to the LORD your God.

JOEL 2:12–14

I sat on my friend's couch, looking at the sweet women in my small group. We were discussing the chapters we'd read in the last week, and it was time.

Nobody would know if I didn't speak up. Though we'd been talking about the parts of the book that had encouraged and convicted us most, they had no idea how God had used one small paragraph to remove the scales from my eyes and pierce my heart with fiery truth. I didn't have to confess. But it was time.

I took a deep breath and blurted it out. I told them how I'd thought of a friend who needed to read a specific point in our book—and how God had straightened me right up, making it clear in my heart that I was the one who needed that message. I told them how He'd brought to mind a situation in which I was the guilty party, in which I had deliberately disobeyed God's commands.

Eyes downcast, I assured them I'd learned my lesson. I apologized, aware that I'd probably disappointed them. Their response was so kind. They understood how hard it can be to love others the way God calls us to. But like the best friends do, they offered accountability alongside their grace and mercy. And in that moment, when they forgave me but didn't excuse my actions, I realized how long it had been since I had sincerely confessed a sin.

Of course, I apologize for mistakes all the time. And certainly, in quiet moments in a church service or the carpool line or the shower, I might be hit with conviction. But in the same breath I utter a quick, "sorry," I immediately move into gratitude for forgiveness and fresh mercies, vowing to try harder and do better next time.

Facing my sin that morning, I saw clearly my need for true confession, for the fasting and weeping and mourning that comes when we recognize just how far from holy we are. Don't get me wrong! I don't think God intends for us to wallow in our regret, to stay stuck in the mud of our mistakes without hope or healing. He is, after all, a God of forgiveness and mercy. He's a God who loves us so much He sent His son to take the punishment for our sins. But if we don't acknowledge our brokenness or the severity of our sins, if we shrug them off as no big deal or assume "it's all good" because we are forgiven, we're missing the point. We're missing the point of what Jesus did for us on the cross, and we're missing the blessing of feeling the weight of our sin lifted off of us.

If it's been a while since confessing your sin caused you to mourn before you rejoiced over God's grace, I invite you to join me in a posture of humble repentance this Lent season. Let's spend the next few weeks reflecting on God's goodness while also taking a hard look at ourselves. And when we see all the ways we fall short of the glory of God, let's not sweep our grief or waywardness under the carpet. Let's be honest about it, and believe that we aren't bearing the burden of them ourselves—God bore them for us on the cross. Let's allow that reality to sink in.

Let us prepare for the wonder of the resurrection by remembering just how much we need it. Let us turn to the Lord with hearts truly broken over our transgressions, more grateful than ever for His abounding love and forgiveness.

God, I'm so sorry. I'm sorry I've taken Your lavish grace for granted, overlooking and underestimating my sin. Please forgive me. Please bring to mind the things I need to confess and give me the courage to turn them over to You. Thank You, Lord, for loving me so much that You died for my every sin. Thank You for not being content to leave me in my mess, for remembering me even when I forget how much I need You. Thank You, Jesus. Amen.

QUESTIONS TO CONSIDER

1. Before you rush onto the next thing today, take a few minutes to ask the Lord to search your heart. When you're quiet and listen for His answer, what do you hear from the Lord?

2. Is it possible to feel both grief over your sin and gratitude over God's forgiveness? How do you hold both responses at once?

_____

_____

_____

_____

_____

3. What would true accountability look like in the area you most struggle? How you can you proactively seek that kind of accountability this week and in the months to come?

_____

_____

_____

_____

_____

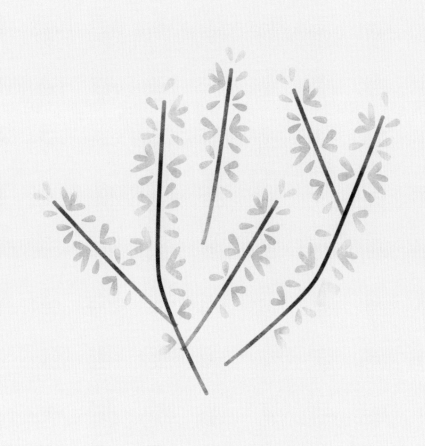

DAY 22
REFLECTION

God is extraordinarily and eternally faithful. When you seek Him, you will find Him. When you confess your sins, He will forgive you. And no matter what you do or where you go, He will love you with an everlasting love. Select one or two of the following Scriptures and meditate on God's faithfulness.

God is not a man, that he might lie, or a son of man, that he might change his mind. Does he speak and not act, or promise and not fulfill?

NUMBERS 23:19

Let us hold on to the confession of our hope without wavering, since he who promised is faithful.

HEBREWS 10:23

Know that the Lord your God is God, the faithful God who keeps his gracious covenant loyalty for a thousand generations with those who love him and keep his commands.

DEUTERONOMY 7:9

The one who conceals his sins will not prosper, but whoever confesses and renounces them will find mercy.

PROVERBS 28:13

But the Lord is faithful; he will strengthen and guard you from the evil one.

2 THESSALONIANS 3:3

For the word of the Lord is right, and all his work is trustworthy.

PSALM 33:4

Because of the Lord's faithful love we do not perish, for his mercies never end. They are new every morning; great is your faithfulness!

LAMENTATIONS 3:22–23

Where have you seen God's faithfulness in the past?

Where do you need to see God's faithfulness today?

Temptation

Then Jesus was led up by the Spirit into the wilderness to be tempted by the devil. After he had fasted forty days and forty nights, he was hungry. Then the tempter approached him and said, "If you are the Son of God, tell these stones to become bread."

He answered, "It is written: Man must not live on bread alone but on every word that comes from the mouth of God."

Then the devil took him to the holy city, had him stand on the pinnacle of the temple, and said to him, "If you are the Son of God, throw yourself down. For it is written:

He will give his angels orders concerning you,
and they will support you with their hands
so that you will not strike
your foot against a stone."

Jesus told him, "It is also written: Do not test the Lord your God."

Again, the devil took him to a very high mountain and showed him all the kingdoms of the world and their splendor. And he said to him, "I will give you all these things if you will fall down and worship me."

Then Jesus told him, "Go away, Satan! For it is written: Worship the Lord your God, and serve only him."

Then the devil left him, and angels came and began to serve him.

MATTHEW 4:1–11

The email came late in the day. I didn't see it until even later that evening, and when I did, I was simultaneously devastated and relieved. After three years of working for a company, I was being notified that my services were no longer needed. My team appreciated my hard work, but in two weeks, we'd go our separate ways. In the meantime I was asked to wrap up loose ends and train the person who would be taking over my tasks.

I felt relief because I'd been longing to quit this job and focus on other opportunities. I had stayed to avoid debt—which now seemed unavoidable, as I held a job loss in one hand and some unexpected bills in the other. Still, a small part of me was happy this decision had been taken out of my hands and I'd no longer have to stay in a position that wasn't really a good fit anymore.

The larger part of my mind, however, found it hard to breathe as panic immediately set in. We had these bills to pay. And we'd been eating out too much and saving too little. And my car was making that noise and the kids kept outgrowing their shoes and the deposit I'd made for that trip was nonrefundable.

What were we going to do?

Why did this happen?

Would God provide this time?

Right away my mind went to worst-case scenarios, and I began making a list of subscriptions to stop and memberships to cancel. Years of struggling financially (often due to my own poor choices) had built strong muscles and ready reflexes. I might not be great at staying on budget, but worry about where we'll find money to pay all our bills? That I can do.

Jesus urges us not to be anxious—about our lives, our needs, or our future (Matthew 6:25–34), but I've always found that easier said than done. Or, perhaps, easier read than obeyed. I'm a planner and a nurturer by nature, so finding myself unable to know for sure if I can take care of all the people and all the things leaves me unsettled at best and spiraling with uncertainty at worst. When control has been wrenched from my hands in those situations, like this one, my strongest urge is to yank the reins by doing the only thing I can: worry.

But worrying like that is disobeying God. Simply put, it's sin. And I know that. He's shown me many times—just as many times as He's proven perfectly capable of taking care of all the things and all the people without my interference or input. Still, I struggle. And that day when I gained a huge medical bill and then lost the job that would have covered it, I turned to the comfort of the familiar. In the face of bad news and doubt, my old friend worry welcomed me with open arms.

Are you a worrier? Do you fight the urge to fret and fuss instead of trust and believe? Or perhaps you've mastered casting all your anxieties on the Lord and depending on Him for your needs. Perhaps your biggest struggle today is something different. Whatever temptation you face today, you are not alone. Every one of us is confronted with the thing we long to do but know we shouldn't, with the thing we've done in the past but have sworn not to do again, with the exact thing we crave most in our weakest moments.

Even Jesus was tempted in the same way.

The gospel of Matthew tells us that after going more than a month without food or water, after spending nearly six weeks in complete isolation, Jesus had to do battle with the devil. He was hungry, and the devil offered bread—tempting Jesus not just to satisfy His hunger but to take control of a situation. Later he offered power and glory, trying to trick Jesus into testing His own Father and worshiping His enemy.

Each time He was met with temptation, Jesus resisted. Though He was weakened from fasting, He leaned on the strength of His Father. Though the devil was sneaky and clever, Jesus leaned on His knowledge of truth in Scripture. And so He resisted temptation while also giving us a template for doing the same.

In the seconds it took to read bad news in an email, I turned to the sin I've struggled with as long as I can remember. But, while I did stumble in that moment, I didn't stay there. Through God's grace (and years of lessons learned the hard way) I remembered the real solution to a problem like this one. I remembered that worry won't add a minute to my life—or a dollar to my bank account. And I remembered that what makes a difference in this and every single situation that arises is looking the devil in the face and resisting just like Jesus. What turns my heart around, even if my circumstances stay the same, is meditating on the Word of God, trusting Him, and worshiping Him with gratitude and awe for who He is and everything He has done and will do.

As we spend this season of Lent letting God prepare our hearts for a celebration of the resurrection, we may find ourselves feeling vulnerable. When we spend time face to face with the magnitude of our God and the depravity of our own sin, when we humble ourselves and repent, when we obey God's call to sacrifice and to serve others, that is likely when temptation will strike hardest. And it's then that we must follow Jesus' blueprint for resistance and leave that devil behind in the wilderness.

Thank you, Jesus. Thank You for facing the devil and refusing to back down. Thank You for looking him in the eye and bowing to no one but God, our Father. Thank You for showing us exactly how to resist the temptation we face every day, not by being superhuman or super strong, but by leaning on the strength we're all given by God. Please protect me. Protect me from every temptation, every sin, every familiar disobedience my instincts tell me to embrace. Give me strength, Lord, and give me clarity to remember Your Word in the right moments. Remind me of all the truth I've learned about you and what you want for me. Help me resist, God. Thank You. I love You. Amen.

What turns my heart around is MEDITATING on the WORD of GOD, TRUSTING HIM, and WORSHIPPING HIM with GRATITUDE and AWE for who He is and everything He has done and will do.

QUESTIONS TO CONSIDER

1. Every single one of us battles temptation of some sort. What specific temptation are you facing today?

_____

_____

_____

_____

_____

_____

2. We are most vulnerable to sin when we are weakened in some way. Where do you need to lean on God's strength in order to resist the devil?

_____

_____

_____

_____

_____

_____

_____

_____

_____

_____

3. What Scripture could you memorize this week that would help you fight temptation just like Jesus did in the desert?

_____

_____

_____

_____

_____

_____

_____

_____

_____

_____

_____

DAY 24
PSALM 136:1–9

Give thanks to the LORD, for he is good.
  His faithful love endures forever.

Give thanks to the God of gods.
  His faithful love endures forever.

Give thanks to the Lord of lords.
  His faithful love endures forever.

He alone does great wonders.
  His faithful love endures forever.

He made the heavens skillfully.
  His faithful love endures forever.

He spread the land on the waters.
  His faithful love endures forever.

He made the great lights:
  His faithful love endures forever.

the sun to rule by day,
  His faithful love endures forever.

the moon and stars to rule by night.
  His faithful love endures forever.

Time Machine

Not that I have already reached the goal or am already perfect, but I make every effort to take hold of it because I also have been taken hold of by Christ Jesus. Brothers and sisters, I do not consider myself to have taken hold of it. But one thing I do: Forgetting what is behind and reaching forward to what is ahead, I pursue as my goal the prize promised by God's heavenly call in Christ Jesus.

PHILIPPIANS 3:12–14

Well, it's nearly spring. January has come and gone. Nobody has asked about your resolutions in weeks, it's possible to find a parking spot at the gym, and on the rare occasion you are required to write the date, your hand automatically draws the correct numbers.

We are fully into the new year now, and yet some of us are still living in the past.

We're not even surprised when we break our resolutions, again. Or we didn't bother making resolutions or setting goals in the first place, because why bother? We look at the hard situation we're facing and think it will never be over, or we wonder if we'll ever be out of the woods. Some of us even find ourselves questioning the good things that are happening. Surely, it was meant for someone else. Or maybe it's not even real. Because we know we don't deserve this.

A couple months ago, I watched the finale to a TV show about time travel. One of the characters spent much of the episode struggling with guilt over his actions in an alternate time line. As he whined—I mean, lamented—to one of the characters he'd hurt with his actions, she lost her patience. She said:

"Why are you beating yourself up over a history that only you and I remember?"

I couldn't shake those words, even as the credits rolled. I started wondering if maybe that's what Jesus is saying to me every time I dwell on the past, forgetting I've been forgiven and remembering every one of my mistakes, my bad decisions, my sins. Even He doesn't remember those things. Psalm 103 says He removes our sins as far as the east is from the west, and Jeremiah 31 says God promises to forgive our sin and never remember it. No, we can't change our past, but God will forgive it. No time machine or alternate time line required.

So why are we sometimes so determined to remember every misstep we've ever taken? Why do we bring to mind the ugly things we've said, the regrettable way we've behaved, the times we let others—and ourselves—down? Why do we hit "play" on that record, over and over again, until every detail is ingrained in our minds where they can't be ignored or forgotten?

In the television show I watched, the two main characters were literally the only people who remembered what had happened and how much it had hurt. In our own lives, reality isn't so kind. But even when forgiveness has been offered and time has begun healing wounds, we tend to hold onto the memory of our mistakes anyway—as if keeping the memories alive is some kind of atonement, rather than abuse. As if accepting forgiveness somehow diminishes our grief and regret. As if we cannot accept forgiveness until we have punished ourselves sufficiently.

Except . . . Jesus.

The One who deliberately does not recall our sins once He's forgiven them? He's the same One who took every bit of punishment we deserve. And He did it so we don't have to. He looked at our dirty, tear-stained faces full of regret or defiance, shame or arrogance, and He loved us anyway—enough to pay the price for it all, in fact. When we asked, He forgave us. And then He washed us clean, white as snow.

So, here we are, stripped bare and standing in the middle of Lent. And we have a choice. Do we move forward into whatever this year has for us, into whatever God has planned for us? Or do we keep looking back at our pasts, circling back to our mistakes, playing the tape of our failures and our faults over and over again?

Let's move forward, friend. Let's trust that when Jesus said, "It is finished," He really meant it! Let's believe that He no longer brings to mind our mistakes, that He's removed our sin and washed us clean. Let's quit beating ourselves up for a past that only we remember.

We don't even need a time machine to do it. We simply need to accept Christ's forgiveness and step forward into our future.

Dear God, Why is it so hard to let go of the past? I believe You when You say I'm forgiven, and yet I can't stop regretting the things that have happened, the things I've done. But I want to. I want to live in freedom from both sin and shame, and I know You can help me do that. Please help me! Help me truly and fully accept Your forgiveness and move forward. Please open my eyes to the good works You still have prepared for me and protect me from shame and the lies of the enemy. Thank You, Lord. Thank You for refusing to "beat me up" over a history that You've paid for and that you now no longer remember. I love You. Amen.

QUESTIONS TO CONSIDER

1. If you had a time machine, would you use it? Where or when would you travel? What would you change?

2. Do you believe God has completely erased your sin? What gets in the way of accepting this kind of forgiveness?

3. What do you think God might do with your life if you could truly let go of what's come before? How would you like to serve Him as you move forward?

"To be grateful is to recognize the love of God in everything He has given us—and He has given us everything. Every breath we draw is a gift of His love, every moment of existence is a grace, for it brings with it immense graces from Him."

—THOMAS MERTON

In his sermon "The Novelties of Divine Mercy," Charles Spurgeon said it well: "The glory of God's faithfulness is that no sin of ours has ever made Him unfaithful." What an incredible gift! What a mercy! Let's take time today, this Lent season, and always, to focus on God's faithfulness and express our deep gratitude for it.

Think about the gift of salvation, about Jesus' sacrifice. Think about your own brokenness. Think about everything that would stand between you and our holy God, and think about just how thankful you are that God loved us enough to bridge that gap and bring you back to Him.

Finished

Jesus said, "It is finished."

JOHN 19:30

A few years ago my church read through the Bible chronologically. As we traveled through the desert with the Israelites and watched them make the same mistakes, over and over and over, I wondered if maybe we're all programmed to repeat history. I wondered if getting stuck in a cycle is inevitable, if it's possible to avoid the experience of looking at a hard situation and realizing that you've been there before, that it's not as new or surprising as you initially thought.

Strangely enough, those Old Testament stories and my wondering made me think of Winnie the Pooh. While Pooh wasn't looking for a new home outside the Hundred Acre Wood, that silly bear and his friends got lost in the woods so many times! In book after book, movie after movie, we saw them wandering around in circles, following their own footprints, jumping at every mysterious sound they hear, passing the same landmarks again and again. Winnie the Pooh and his friends were just as lost and confused as the Israelites. And they were just as mixed up and frightened as I am in the same scenario.

Now, I certainly don't mean that I've spent decades lost in the same forest. Not literally, at least. I've never been haunted by howls or Heffalumps; I've never been chased by mysterious animals or gotten so hungry for honey that I begin hallucinating. But have I ever crawled to the end of one race only to be tossed into the middle of another one? Have I ever faced trial after trial after trial until it feels like I'm crawling through mud, like I'm dragging myself through the miry clay? Have I wandered away from the path God made for me, following my own desires and dreams instead of His? *Oh yeah.*

Sometimes I'm lost because I'm an Israelite at heart, returning to the same fear and pride and anger that got me in trouble in the first place. When that happens I'm almost always slow to recognize the pattern of my own sin, the responsibility I own for my stress. And even once I do, figuring out how to break the cycle can seem just as difficult and exhausting as sitting and suffering in the sin.

Sometimes I find myself [metaphorically] in the woods because this life is hard, because circumstances are out of my control and, seemingly, out to get me. And sometimes saying, "when it rains, it pours," doesn't even come close to describing the mind-numbing weariness that comes with one hard situation after another, with a season determined to illustrate Jesus' claim that we will certainly face tribulation in this life.

And sometimes we face a situation that is unlike our previous experience but shares enough characteristics with something that's hurt us or something we've struggled with in the past that it brings it all up again. And we find ourselves thinking: *Aren't we out of the woods yet? How can we be lost again? Aren't we over this thing?*

But not only did Jesus predict that we would face trouble in this world, He declared that He has overcome this world. And when He was breathing His last breaths on the cross, He answered our desperate cries once and for all. "It is finished," He cried.

It is finished. Though we may feel dizzy with the tribulations of this world, Jesus has promised—both in word and in beautiful, blood-spilling deed—that while we may have started the cycle of sin and entered the proverbial woods of this world, He has finished it. He has borne the weight of every one of our sins, every ounce of mud, every dark corner of the woods, every toss of the cruel wind. He took it all, and He rose victorious. He faced our fears and our doubts and our sin, and He won. It might not feel like it yet, but we know the war is over.

It is finished.

He has borne the weight of every one of our sins, every ounce of mud, every dark corner of the woods, every toss of the cruel wind. He took it all, & He rose victorious.

Remember, when you face something that feels achingly familiar, it will not torment you forever. We know how our every story ends and who wins the war; God wrote the ending when His Son gave His life for ours. All our reflection and repentance, our sacrifice and serving, our humbling and hoping—it's all led us here, to the cross. Lent has prepared us to arrive at the very moment where Jesus took our place in the desperate, doomed battle against the woods and won, where He declared, "It is finished."

It is finished. Our time in the wilderness and the woods is over. Our Lord has died, for us, but He's risen again. And it is finished.

Oh Lord, I am overwhelmed. The thought of You taking the punishment for my sin, the thought of You fighting my every battle—I'm overcome with gratitude, Lord! I am not worthy, but I am thankful. And I'm relieved. I'm relieved to know I won't be bombarded with the tribulations of this world forever. I'm relieved to know I don't have to fight this war, that You've already won, that even if it doesn't feel like it yet, I know You finished this battle once and for all. Thank You, Jesus! Thank You. I love You. Amen.

QUESTIONS TO CONSIDER

1. Has your life ever felt like the Hundred Acre Wood? Have you ever felt like the Israelites wandering in the wilderness? How so?

_____

_____

_____

_____

2. Who or what do you turn to when you feel lost or confused or weary?

_____

_____

_____

_____

3. What is one way you can anchor your heart in truth, so it always points to God and the reminder that our struggles on earth won't last forever?

_____

_____

_____

_____

_____

DAY 28
REFLECTION

As we near the cross and our celebration of the resurrection, let us look forward to spring, to a season of new growth and fresh mercies, to a time of renewed devotion and determination to resist temptation and remember what we've learned during this time of Lent.

When we study Jesus' time in the wilderness, we learn that one of His main strategies to resist Satan's temptations was using His knowledge of both God and Scripture. And when Paul shares the promise in Philippians that God will guard our hearts and minds, he suggests that, in order to stay away from sin, we focus on things that are true, honorable, just, pure, lovely, commendable, and praiseworthy. So let's do just that.

Look around. What do you see that is lovely?

_____

_____

_____

Listen for good news instead of the bad today. What can you find that is honorable and just?

_____

_____

_____

Reflect on the nature of God. What about Him is true? What makes Him so incredibly worthy of our praise?

_____

_____

_____

What are some favorite Scripture passages that encourage you to remain faithful to God? Who could you share these passages with?

_____

_____

_____

How do you think focusing on these things will help you resist temptation?

_____

_____

_____

What have you learned this Lent season by studying Jesus' time in the wilderness?

_____

_____

_____

DAY 29

DEVOTION

Fresh Starts

Because of the LORD's faithful love
we do not perish,
for his mercies never end.
They are new every morning;
great is your faithfulness!

LAMENTATIONS 3:22–23

As we ate our takeout and queued up our shows on the DVR, my husband and I caught up on the business of the week. We talked *again* about our daughter's behavior, and I confessed something I'd realized about the situation. "I can't start fresh," I whispered. "My frustrations just keep building and building, and there's no break, no relief, no blank slate."

The conversations about our daughter's disobedience and disrespect began bringing other issues to the table—namely, our tempers. We realized that our short fuses were contributing to the problem, but we didn't know how to fix it. And I knew that this fresh start thing was part of it.

Without a fresh start, there's no forgiveness. And without forgiveness, I couldn't find my way out of the garbage heap of anger. I couldn't see the light of grace.

Of course, everyone says that admitting your problem is the first step—and it is. But even though this realization—and the courage to describe it out loud to my husband—felt huge, it wasn't enough. I needed to make a change for our family. I needed to do something different.

I wish I could say that difference happened naturally, on its own, that somehow I magically learned how to forgive and forget and shower my child and myself with grace.

But that wouldn't be true.

What happened instead was that I kept feeling angry and frustrated; I kept losing my temper with my disobedient, disrespectful little girl. And I kept remembering that I am part of the problem. I would put her to bed, so mad at the latest argument and so glad to be finished with the day, and then I would cry because I didn't know how to stop feeling that way.

But then as I lamented our struggle to her first-grade teacher, something did change. My daughter's teacher suggested we use the same color-coded behavior chart at home that they use in the classroom. I knew several months into this school year how important the color chart was to my daughter.

Every afternoon, her response to my question, "How was your day?" was what color she was on: A green day was good, average, normal, nothing to see here. A yellow (or even red) day meant she was crying before she even got in the car. A blue or pink day, though, was cause for celebration—high fives and hugs all around!

We'd made a half-hearted attempt to use a color chart at home before, and it didn't help at all. But at this point, I was not just angry and frustrated; I was disappointed in myself and a little desperate for help.

And it worked. *It worked!* But not for the reasons I expected.

See, at school the colors came with consequences, and the good colors came with prizes. Plus, students had the added incentive of their classmates knowing where they stood each day. But none of that was in play at home. I wasn't about to give out prizes for simple obedience, and her baby sister didn't care what color my daughter was on.

What made the difference was that at the end of the day, no matter how ugly or difficult or red it was, I moved my daughter's pin back to green. Every day started at green. Every day started fresh, blank, clean. It had the potential to be better or worse, but it started on green.

Something about physically moving that clothespin back to the green spot on our laminated color chart reset my heart, too. Even after the worst days, that simple gesture lifted a burden from my heart. Moving my daughter's pin back to green let me breathe again. It helped me love her better, again. And it reminded me that because of God's great mercy I get to start on green each day, too.

Though I struggle to be a good mom some days (or some years), God is the perfect heavenly Father. So it should have been no surprise that His methods work for me, too. God promises to wipe our slate clean, to remove our sin as far as the east is from the west. In the sacrifice of Jesus Christ, He offers us an abundance of mercy—and then He promises to refill that overflowing cup every single day.

Part of the Lent season is humbling ourselves. It is lowering our defenses and our pride, allowing God to strip away our sin and our distractions. It's the grueling work of meaning it when we say, "more of you, less of me," to our holy and mighty God. But though we begin this season there, God doesn't leave us in our guilt and shame. He doesn't force us out of the garden, naked and trembling. No, instead, He reaches for us and covers us in His grace. He erases every sin we confess and loves us through the entire process.

Just like my daughter gets to start on green, so do we. Even when we're our most disobedient, we are forgiven. And we get to start over again. When we're washed clean by the blood of Jesus, we get a fresh start. What a precious gift!

Heavenly Father, thank You for loving me so much better than I can ever love my own children. Thank You for adopting me into Your family and loving me even when I'm as disobedient as a child! And thank You for forgiving my every sin, wiping the slate clean, and giving me a fresh start each day. Because, Lord, I mess up every day. I need Your grace every day. And I'm so grateful for it! Thank You, God. I love you. Amen.

QUESTIONS TO CONSIDER

1. Do you ever struggle to offer fresh mercies to yourself or to others?

_____

_____

_____

_____

_____

_____

_____

_____

2. What can you do today to get "back to green," to begin new?

_____

_____

_____

_____

_____

_____

3. Have you asked God to forgive your sins, to give Him the opportunity to lavish you with fresh mercies and grace today? If not, what holds you back?

_____

_____

_____

_____

_____

_____

DAY 30
PRAYER

Dear God,

You are so faithful, so generous, so gracious. Your gift of salvation can sometimes feel overwhelming when I consider my own faithlessness, my own fallibility, my own foolishness. I can barely breathe when I think that You created the heavens and earth but are also mindful of me. I can hardly believe it when I think that You loved me so much that You paid the price of my sin. But, Lord, I do believe! I believe and I am so thankful. I'm so thankful that You love me, so thankful that You didn't leave me in my sin, so thankful that You refuse to let anything come between us.

Forgive me, Lord, for all the times I've forgotten—about Your greatness, about Your grace, about You. Forgive me for putting myself first, and thank You for being faithful to remind me, time and again, of the plans You have for me and the path You've laid for me. Thank You for giving me an example to follow in Jesus and Your Word as a weapon to use when I face temptation. Thank You for forgiving me, again, when I stumble. And thank You for being so faithful to me when I fail, while never seeing me as a failure.

God, I love You so much. Thank You for loving me.

Amen.

DAY 31

DEVOTION

Learn More

After six days Jesus took Peter, James, and John and led them up a high mountain by themselves to be alone. He was transfigured in front of them, and his clothes became dazzling—extremely white as no launderer on earth could whiten them. Elijah appeared to them with Moses, and they were talking with Jesus. Peter said to Jesus, "Rabbi, it's good for us to be here. Let us set up three shelters: one for you, one for Moses, and one for Elijah"—because he did not know what to say, since they were terrified.

A cloud appeared, overshadowing them, and a voice came from the cloud: "This is my beloved Son; listen to him!"

Suddenly, looking around, they no longer saw anyone with them except Jesus.

As they were coming down the mountain, he ordered them to tell no one what they had seen until the Son of Man had risen from the dead. They kept this word to themselves, questioning what "rising from the dead" meant.

MARK 9:2–10

Have you ever been certain you were following God's will, only to be completely shocked by an unexpected turn of events that pushed you in a different direction? Or maybe you've thought you finally understood something—something about the world or the Lord or yourself—only to realize that you actually don't have a clue?

I've been there—and so have the disciples.

When Jesus took Peter, James, and John up to the mountain, they'd already spent quite a bit of time together. The disciples had seen Jesus perform many miracles, they'd heard Him teaching with authority, and Peter had even declared that Jesus was the Christ.

They probably thought they had a pretty good grasp on who Jesus was and what His mission was. But if you've read the Gospels, you already know that despite all the time the disciples had spent with Jesus, they had a hard time comprehending the full picture of His identity and ministry. Though they saw Him heal the sick and turn water to wine, though they watched Him walk on water and calm storms, they still doubted. They still questioned. They still said things they undoubtedly regretted later.

They still weren't sure of who He was, and they certainly didn't understand why He did the things He did.

According to the Scriptures, Peter was a frequent player in the game of awkward statements and careless actions—wearing his heart on his sleeve, speaking before thinking, and generally blurting out everything that came to his mind. I especially appreciate how the author of this story is so honest, saying that Peter said what he did because he was scared and didn't know what to say. Never one to stand down when faced with confusion, he spoke up anyway and illustrated just how much he still didn't know about Jesus.

As we're walking through this season of reflection together, I'm thinking about how often I've read a passage in the Bible or listened to a sermon and thought, "Yep, yep, I totally get it. I hear you, Lord! I've got this," only to realize at a later date how incomplete or even incorrect my understanding was. Over and over, I learn that the only way for me to truly know God is by spending more time with Him.

And when I consider what "more time" means, I think about the disciples. Those men spent time with Jesus every day; they observed Him up close and personal! But still, they needed deeper conversations and literal mountaintop experiences to fully comprehend their friend and Savior.

So do we.

My five-year-old is currently obsessed with how much each of us knows. She has accepted that only God knows everything, but she asks who knows more, Mommy or Daddy. She understands that she goes to school to learn more, but she can't quite grasp why her dad and I say we still have a lot to learn. You can see her wondering, *Haven't they learned all they're going to learn by now? What could they possibly have left to learn? And if they're still learning, are they eventually going to know everything?*

We chuckle at her innocent questions and do our best to explain what most of us honestly struggle with as well. Yes, we know some things. No, we don't know all things. Yes, we want to keep learning. No, we will never be finished learning.

No matter how long we've known the Lord, we still have SO MUCH to learn AND so many WAYS to GROW.

It's really as basic as that—for a preschooler, for the disciples, and for us. No matter how long we've known the Lord (or how very old we might be in the eyes of a child!), we still have so much to learn and so many ways to grow. And intentionally setting aside a season of reflection and preparation in the days leading up to Easter is a great way to do just that.

Dear Lord, You are so mighty and powerful and truly complex. Forgive me for oversimplifying You and assuming my elementary understanding of You is enough. I know that one day You will reveal everything and I'll realize how much I've misunderstood or just plain missed. But I don't want to wait for that day to learn more about You! I want to know You, God. I want to keep learning. I want to recognize Your voice and know Your heart; I want to be Your friend. I love You, Lord. Please open my eyes and draw me close during this time of Lent. Amen.

QUESTIONS TO CONSIDER

1. When was the last time you were surprised by learning something new about God?

2. Do you intentionally make room to learn more about the Lord? In this season of seeking God, what Bible study could you read or what message series could you listen to in order to do this?

_____

_____

_____

_____

_____

_____

3. What is one question you still have about God? Where or how could you seek deeper understanding in this area?

_____

_____

_____

_____

_____

_____

_____

_____

DAY 32
REFLECTION

Sometimes it can feel like the more we learn, the more we realize we don't know. The journey to the cross can be intense at times, drawing our eyes to a great and mighty God while also making us increasingly aware of our desperate need for His grace and mercy. But we must be determined to let our knowledge—both of the Lord and our own lack—draw us nearer to Him in honor and praise, awe and respect rather than creating any distance between us.

Do you feel closer to God today than you did before observing Lent this year?

_____

_____

_____

Have you learned anything about God that surprised you?

_____

_____

_____

_____

Have you learned anything about yourself that surprised you?

If you are closer to the Lord or more knowledgeable of Him in some way, how will you move forward—to the cross, the resurrection, and beyond?

DAY 33
DEVOTION

Best Days

I am sure of this, that he who started a good work in you will carry it on to completion until the day of Christ Jesus.

PHILIPPIANS 1:6

A couple years ago I went to my twentieth high school reunion. It was an event that I'd built up to be *a thing* in my head, one I was both nervous about and looking forward to. It turned out to be less "a thing" and more a pleasant evening spent with a handful of people I have much affection for and haven't seen in several years.

I grew up in a small town and graduated with just under one hundred people, the majority of whom I'd known since preschool or kindergarten. We certainly didn't spend those formative years always holding hands and singing *Kumbaya*, but overall we were a pretty tight-knit group of kids for most of our young lives. Social media provides a surface-level knowledge of what everyone is up to (or at least what their kids look like), but there's something to be said about putting your arms around an old friend and hugging her neck.

It was a fun night that included some reminiscing, some revelations, and lots of hugs and laughter. I'm glad I went (and may have volunteered to help plan a bigger, better event when we do it again in five years).

However. One moment did surprise me—*and not in a good way.*

A classmate's wife walked up to me pretty early in the evening. I'd said hello when they arrived but hadn't had a chance to chat yet. She stopped in front of me and said, "So, my husband tells me you were the class valedictorian." A little taken aback by her tone and not sure where this conversation was going, I said, "Yes, I was." She then said the very words that I ask myself in my lowest moments. She said, with a big laugh as if we were all in on the joke, "Well, what have you done with that since graduation?"

What have you done?

What have you accomplished?

Is this the best you could do?

You didn't really go anywhere, huh?

Guessed you peaked in high school . . .

In her defense, she didn't say any of those last words, the words that echo in my heart when I doubt myself most. And I don't believe her insult was actually intentional or personal. After all, we hadn't met before that night.

But it sure landed a blow anyway.

High school, for me, was a long time ago. For you it might have been more recent or perhaps you're more years removed than I am. But I don't believe any of our stories ended there. Whether we are exactly where we planned to be or so far from our adolescent dreams that our high school self wouldn't even recognize us now, those days were just a starting point.

Maybe for you high school wasn't anything spectacular; maybe it was traumatic or something you barely survived. I don't believe your story ended there, either. And, really, in the big picture of our lives, graduating high school is just one of many milestones we pass over time.

Going to college, getting a job, being fired from a job, getting married, getting divorced, having kids, losing loved ones, moving away, getting the diagnosis, buying a house, getting a degree, winning a contest, finishing a race, starting a business—our lives have dozens of big moments and new chapters, hundreds of beautiful and terrible milestones, and everything in between. And at each of those points, our stories may have changed or pivoted or been stretched in some way, but they didn't end.

Do you feel disappointed by what you've accomplished this far?

Did you think you'd do more or be different at this point in your life?

Are you afraid that you missed your turn, that you're wasting your potential, that your best days are behind you?

Friend, I promise that's not true. Your story—the one written by the Author of life, the Creator of the world—isn't finished yet. No matter where you find yourself today, no matter what makes up your backstory, no matter how many failures or successes you've experienced, no matter how many milestones you've reached, you have so much more to look forward to. You're just getting started! And God has promised that He will never stop working in us and through us.

I don't know who might be whispering lies into your ear today. I don't know what your specific doubts or fears are, what makes you feel most self-conscious, what you're most afraid of hearing from a stranger or a friend or yourself. But I know this: You are not a failure, and you are not a disappointment. You are just getting started, and God isn't finished with you.

Your best days are yet to come.

Dear God, Creator and Author of every story, thank You for writing a story just for me. Thank You for being an omnipotent Creator, the One who knows every possibility, every turn, every path. Thank You for never giving up on me and for pointing me toward a new story when the one I've been following comes to an end. Thank You for using me in Your grand plan! Please protect me from insecurity that my story might be over, and open my eyes to every opportunity You are placing in front of me, every chance You want me to take, and every change You want me to make. Please guide me, God. I love You and am so grateful to be one part of Your greater story. Thank You, Lord. I love You. Amen.

QUESTIONS TO CONSIDER

1. Has anyone ever said something that made you fear you would no longer have opportunities to serve the Lord? What was that like?

---

2. What helps you remember that God is still working in your heart and your life, that He's still using you and your life?

_____

_____

_____

_____

_____

_____

_____

_____

3. What opportunities are in front of you right now? How can you serve God in a new way?

_____

_____

_____

_____

_____

_____

_____

_____

DAY 34
PSALM 145

I exalt you, my God the King, and bless your name
    forever and ever.
I will bless you every day; I will praise your name
    forever and ever.

The Lord is great and is highly praised; his greatness
    is unsearchable.
One generation will declare your works to the next
    and will proclaim your mighty acts.
I will speak of your splendor and glorious majesty
    and your wondrous works.
They will proclaim the power of your awe-inspiring
    acts, and I will declare your greatness.
They will give a testimony of your great goodness
    and will joyfully sing of your righteousness.

The Lord is gracious and compassionate, slow to
    anger and great in faithful love.
The Lord is good to everyone; his compassion rests
    on all he has made.
All you have made will thank you, Lord; the faithful
    will bless you.
They will speak of the glory of your kingdom and
    will declare your might,
informing all people of your mighty acts and of the
    glorious splendor of your kingdom.

Your kingdom is an everlasting kingdom; your rule
is for all generations.
The LORD is faithful in all his words and gracious in
all his actions.

The LORD helps all who fall; he raises up all who are
oppressed.
All eyes look to you, and you give them their food
at the proper time.
You open your hand and satisfy the desire of every
living thing.

The LORD is righteous in all his ways and faithful in
all his acts.
The LORD is near all who call out to him, all who call
out to him with integrity.
He fulfills the desires of those who fear him; he
hears their cry for help and saves them.
The LORD guards all those who love him, but he
destroys all the wicked.
My mouth will declare the LORD's praise; let every
living thing bless his holy name forever and ever.

Obey Calling

But be doers of the word and not hearers only, deceiving yourselves. Because if anyone is a hearer of the word and not a doer, he is like someone looking at his own face in a mirror. For he looks at himself, goes away, and immediately forgets what kind of person he was. But the one who looks intently into the perfect law of freedom and perseveres in it, and is not a forgetful hearer but a doer who works—this person will be blessed in what he does.

JAMES 1:22–25

I have this cat, Peanut. She's really sweet and affectionate and gentle with children. But she is also just about the most annoying thing on the planet. She talks a lot—and by talking, I mean she chatters and squeaks and meows—but that's not really the problem. In a house full of big talkers, I can hardly complain about that.

The thing that drives me up the wall about Peanut is that she is stubborn. Or lazy. Or both. I'm not really sure where the issue stems from, and I don't have time for kitty therapy. All I know is that when I try to make her move—off my spot on the couch, off the dining room chairs at dinner time, off my leg when I'm trying to sleep at night— she refuses.

For all her flaws, I still love her. So when I want Peanut to move, I'm gentle. I nudge her with my foot or pat her nicely on the back. But most of the time, she won't even deign to open more than one eye at my request. So I move onto more urgent forms of communication. My nudges and pats get a little more aggressive.

Still, nothing moves that cat. In fact, when I attempt to do so, she often raises her head and yells at me. "MROWWWW!" she shouts, indignantly, as if I'm severely inconveniencing her by, you know, wanting to sit on my own couch.

Obviously I'm the human and she's the cat, and eventually she's forced to move. But she makes sure—every single time—to let me know how very unhappy she is about it. It's annoying. And, as sheepish as I am to admit this, it's very similar to how I behave when God asks me to move. Perhaps these scenarios sound familiar to you, too:

Get up early to read my Bible?

But, God, it's just so hard!

Reach out to that person who makes me feel uncomfortable?

But God! It's so awkward! And I don't like being awkward!

Apply for that job? Quit that job? Start that project? Move to that city? Stay here?

But, but, but . . . God! Do I have to? It's so hard!

Try this new thing? Go to a new place? Talk to a new person?

Oh, I don't know. I like how things are now. It's comfy here, easy even. No, thanks . . .

It doesn't really matter what God asks of me. From small changes to big risks, my first instinct is to dig my claws into the couch and stay put, so to speak. Change is hard, and my comfort zone is soft and safe. So when He asks me to follow, my immediate response isn't always one of obedience.

Nope, I can be as stubborn—and, let's be honest, as lazy—as my cat. And that's why I desperately need a season like Lent, where I'm reminded of Christ, who received and obeyed His mission—to come into the world and save it at great cost to Himself—without one word of protest. Yes, I desperately need this season to allow God to strip the sin from my life and prepare me for the works He has for me. This season is a time of humbling and sacrifice, but also a time of preparation. Just like Jesus spent time in the wilderness to prepare for His ministry, the time we dedicate to God during Lent is meant to propel us into action.

When it comes to this Lent season, I'm trying to listen right away and move in the way God is asking. It's not easy, and sometimes I still act like my grumpy, stubborn cat. Like Peanut, I can be resistant to God's

Lent is a time of HUMBLING and SACRIFICE, but also a time of PREPARATION.

nudging. To combat this, I often pray that He will use His Word and my time in prayer to give me the kick in the pants I need to move. I pray He keeps me mindful that no matter what feels safest to me in any given situation, the call to follow Him, to trust Him, and to obey Him is more important than my comfort.

Have you ever struggled to respond to God's nudging? To be a hearer and not a doer of what He's asking of you? Do you have a hard time leaving your comfort zone when God calls? Let's pray that He uses this season of Lent to prepare our hearts for whatever He has planned for us. And when He answers, let's move.

Dear God, forgive me. Forgive me for all the times I've been like a stubborn pet, oblivious to Your plans and refusing to move. Forgive me for being afraid to follow Your call, for being a hearer of the Word but not a doer. Lord, I want to be like Jesus when I'm sent an assignment from You. I want to move on it! I want to put my faith into action . . . but it's hard. If I'm honest, I'm scared of the things You're asking me to do. But I don't want to walk away from this time with You and forget what You've taught me. Please help me obey. Give me courage and strength to answer Your every call. Help me put into action the love that You've shown me. Thank You, Lord. I love You. Amen

QUESTIONS TO CONSIDER

1. What's your first reaction when you feel God asking you to make a change or a move?

2. Is God asking you to make any changes or make any moves right now? How does that make you feel?

3. What is one small step you could take in obedience right now, right away?

DAY 36
GRATITUDE JOURNALING

Is God leading you somewhere new? Is He using this season of fewer distractions and increased devotion to move you out of complacency and onto a different path? Even if you are terrified by what God seems to be whispering in your heart, it is truly amazing to realize that the God of this universe has a unique plan for your life. It is incredible to hear His call to serve Him in a specific way, as well as recognizing all the ways He's been preparing you for such a time and purpose as this.

Let's take time to thank Jesus for all the ways He's prepared us for the calling He's given us. Let's thank Him for fulfilling His own calling so well—the mission of coming to save us all. Let's thank Him for wanting to use us in His grand plan, for wanting to take us on the greatest adventure we could imagine. And let's thank Him for giving us the courage and strength and wisdom we will need every step of the way.

Jump In

Then Jesus came with them to a place called Gethsemane, and he told the disciples, "Sit here while I go over there and pray." Taking along Peter and the two sons of Zebedee, he began to be sorrowful and troubled. He said to them, "I am deeply grieved to the point of death. Remain here and stay awake with me."

Going a little farther, he fell facedown and prayed, "My Father, if it is possible, let this cup pass from me. Yet not as I will, but as you will."

MATTHEW 26:36–39

After a year of recovering from a broken leg—ten months that included two casts and a boot; a wheelchair, walker, and crutches; and more doctor's appointments and physical therapy sessions than I can count—my oldest daughter was finally ready to start exercising again. We considered basketball and karate, but both intimidated my girl. Finally, we decided on swimming. With the goal of regaining enough strength and stamina to make it on a summer swim team, she began swim lessons at the community center.

It's gone pretty well so far, with my tall tween outswimming the younger kids in her beginner class after just a few sessions. And after a year of so many challenges and struggles, she's really enjoyed her reunion with the pool (and her ability to accomplish a goal). Despite her enthusiasm, though, my daughter still hasn't progressed to the next level of classes.

She's a star student every week, following instructions and doing her best as they learn basic swimming techniques. But when it comes time for the students to practice diving into the deep end or jumping off the diving board, she digs in her feet, shakes her head and says, simply, "No."

Ah, yes, that's my stubborn girl.

"Just jump in!" I tell her. "It will be fun! I promise."

"Have I ever told you to do something that hurt you?" I ask.

"What is my job?" I prompt. "Right. My job is to keep you safe. Jumping in is safe!"

"And so fun," adds my husband. "I love jumping in! You'll love it too."

I've gotten so frustrated, watching her across the pool, shaking her head and mouthing to me, "Nooooooooo." Before every lesson, we've talked about diving and jumping in—and how it will be fun and she should do it. She agrees, reluctantly, and I think, *Yes. Today will be the day!*

But it's not. It's not the day, and we are back where we started. And I feel disappointed that she's not doing this great thing that she's supposed to do, this thing that she'll love doing, this thing that she's here to learn. I'm frustrated that she won't believe me, that she doesn't trust me.

And I wonder if this is how God feels about me sometimes.

"Just jump in!" He says. "It will be great, I promise."

"I will always keep you safe," He says, "and besides, this will be so much fun."

"Why won't you do this? This thing I made you to do? Why won't you trust me?"

Sometimes I think I'm pretty brave, but when the Lord puts a new mission in my heart, I feel anything but brave. I feel overwhelmed and under-qualified and unprepared. But mostly, I feel scared. The [metaphorical] pool is big and it might be deep and it's probably cold and I'm just not sure anyone will catch me if I jump.

I don't want to be a scared little girl, afraid to jump, missing out on the amazing thing God has for me, but sometimes a calling can feel like it's just too much. It can feel too big, too hard, too different, too heavy. Sometimes I want to paddle back to the shallow end of the pool, where it's safe and easy and comfortable. But I know that God has more for me—and for you.

If you are overwhelmed by what you believe God is calling you to right now, by the way He seems to be stretching you and challenging you in this season, you're not alone. I, too, have felt my shoulders break under the weight of what I know to be a calling from the Lord. Not just an expectation but a purpose. It can be too much at times, too hard, too demanding, too scary. Just too much.

When both kids are sick at once—and then they swap germs and ailments . . .

When you get a series of hateful comments or emails, criticizing your work (and your heart) . . .

When the event you spent months planning is a flop and only a handful of people show up . . .

When the words won't come or the laundry keeps coming or the deadlines fly by or the tears won't stop . . .

Our callings can feel terrifying, overwhelming, unbearable.

Certainly, we will experience times when we can't stop grinning and glowing, feeling God's pleasure as we run the very race He's given us. We will celebrate and cry buckets of happy tears and know the peace that comes with seeing Him work in our lives. But other times? That calling we were so excited to answer, that purpose we were so thrilled to fulfill? It will be so heavy we think it might just crush us this time.

When it all piles up, when we can't see our way past deadlines and dentist appointments, sick kids and complaint cards, overdue bills and birthday parties, that's when we find ourselves at the end of ourselves. It's when we feel like my daughter, eyes wide and whispering, "No. No! I can't do this. I can't! *Please don't make me do this!*"

If God has CALLED you to LOVE your NEIGHBOR, to SERVE your FAMILY, to MINISTER to your COMMUNITY, (and He has), then He is WITH you every step of the way.

Perhaps you've stayed strong and overcome challenges and faced down enemies and ignored critics, only to realize that this thing you're battling today might be the one thing you can't defeat. If that's where you find yourself today, you're not alone.

And it's no accident that God called you, the weak or weary or unprepared or overwhelmed, to this thing. After all, Jesus Himself in His greatest mission and calling—the cross and the resurrection—was weak and weary, too. Yet He relied on the Father for strength, and He saw His calling through. Just as He was with Jesus, if God has called you to love your neighbor, to serve your family, to minister to your community (and He has), then He is with you every step of the way, too—even the tentative steps, the shuffling steps, the can't-take-another-step steps. Just like He gave Moses, a poor speaker, the words to say to Pharaoh, God will provide exactly what you need when you need it. Just like Moses found friends to hold up his arms when he no longer could do it on his own, God will send people to answer His calling alongside you.

We are not alone, though our callings are as unique as we are. And though our callings might never be easy or comfortable, they will always be worth it. God has called us to dive in and no matter how many deep ends we face, He will be with us. He will be with us, and we can do this. He will be with you, and you can do this.

Dear God, I'm not sure I can do this. I want to be brave; I want to follow You boldly wherever you call me to go. But it's hard, and I'm scared. Help me. Please help me bear this burden and embrace this opportunity. Help me follow you—to strange lands, through hard seasons, and even right into the deep end! Thank you for using me as part of Your plan to bring people back to You. Thank You for calling me, though I'm weak and foolish. Thank You for what You're going to do in my life, Lord. I love You. Amen.

QUESTIONS TO CONSIDER

1. Have you ever dug in your feet and refused to move, out of fear? How did that situation end or resolve itself?

_____

_____

_____

_____

_____

_____

_____

_____

_____

_____

2. Can you think of a time when you jumped right into the [metaphorical] pool, bravely following where the Lord led you? What was it like? How did God show up for you?

_____

_____

_____

_____

_____

_____

3. If you're afraid to dive in right now, or if you're afraid you might drown any minute now, what do you need to remember about God's plan for you (and His love for you)? What habits can you put in place to keep calling these truths to mind?

_____

_____

_____

_____

_____

_____

DAY 38

REFLECTION

The idea of a calling can be hard to comprehend, but it's not meant to be mysterious. Listening for and following God's call doesn't necessarily mean selling everything you own, abandoning everything you've known, and moving across the ocean or even across town. God is infinitely creative, and He's made a unique plan for each of us.

But what we do know—and have in common—is God's universal call for us to acknowledge His holiness as well as our own sin, to understand that we are incapable of paying the price required to be forgiven of that sin, and to believe that Jesus made Himself the sacrifice so we could once again be in fellowship with God. After all, the good news of Easter is that Jesus not only paid the penalty for our sins, which was death, but He also overcame death and rose! The power of sin, and the penalty for it, had no hold on Him. He got out of the grave and invites us to one day do the same, if we will only believe. Indeed, He calls us to confess our sins and believe in His work on the cross and the resurrection, and once we do, to share the good news with those around us, and to seek Him and His will for our lives from now on.

Have you done that? Would you like to?

What has the Lord been saying to you during Lent?

_____

_____

_____

What do you believe He is asking you to do in response?

_____

_____

_____

What do you think God is preparing you to do next?

_____

_____

_____

What do you need in order to take steps in following Him?

_____

_____

_____

_____

DAY 39
DEVOTION

In the Blood

I am able to do all things through him who strengthens me.

PHILIPPIANS 4:13

My oldest is ten years old, officially a "tween," as she's informed me. I suppose this means a lot of things, but one of the most fun is that as her mom, I have a legitimate reason to listen to pop music. Unironically. That's what she likes, so that's what we listen to, along with my playlists of show tunes, worship songs, country music, and what has somehow become "oldies." I'm listening to the music with her and because of her, and that's a parenting perk I'm happy to receive.

One of my daughter's favorite artists released a new song recently. She was excited to hear it come on the radio, but as I caught some of the lyrics coming out of our car's speakers, I was relieved we were pulling into our garage. While I might be able to convince myself I'm a cool mom who listens to cool music, all street cred flies out the window when I begin openly weeping at lines written by nineteen-year-old pop stars.

A few days later, I heard the entire song while alone in the car, and sure enough, I teared up. Amidst cries for help and descriptions of anxiety or depression or some other unnamed but relatable struggle, the singer repeats these words:

> Sometimes I feel like giving up
> But I just can't
> It isn't in my blood

The tears that lined my face weren't the result of sadness for the pop star on my radio. I cried because I feel that truth in my own life, in my own family. Every single one of us—on every side, on every branch—struggles with something or some things. And yet we don't give up. We fight. We keep going. Not always immediately or well or happily, but giving up isn't in my blood.

I thought about that as I nodded my head to the song, tapping my steering wheel for emphasis. *Yes! I'm strong! That's who I am!* I thought proudly.

And then I thought about my daughter, who spent months recuperating from a broken leg last year. I thought about how incredibly hard her experience was (for both of us), how painful it was to encourage her and motivate her and watch her give up over and over again. I thought about how many times I snapped in that season, yelling that she is not allowed to say the word *can't* anymore. And then

I thought about how this song is the exact thing I've been trying to tell her—that she can't *can't*, that she can't give up, that she can't be anything other than strong and fierce and brave.

After all, it's not in my blood, and it's not in hers.

But then new tears sprang up for a completely different reason. I thought about how many times I have, in fact, given up and quit, how many times I have been anything other than strong or fierce or brave. And I remembered that even when I couldn't stand on my own or take another step or handle one more blow, it was okay.

The truth is that giving up actually is in my blood. I'm just as weak and fallible and human as the next person. And just like all the pep talks and motivational posters and fight songs and inspiring books can't force my daughter to face challenges with strength and courage, nothing can change my own tendency to run away, to give up, to quit. I can't will either one of us into new personalities, new abilities, new DNA.

Long after I listened to that song, the chorus played in my head on a loop, weaving in and out of my thoughts. The more those lyrics wove through my brain, the more the word blood rang in my ears and my heart. And then the tune changed, and I remembered another song about blood:

> Would you be free from the burden of sin?
> There's power in the blood, power in the blood;
> Would you o'er evil a victory win?
> There's wonderful power in the blood.
> There is power, power, wonder-working power
> In the blood of the Lamb.

> There is power, power, wonder-working power
> In the precious blood of the Lamb.

In what might be the strangest mash-up of our day, I suddenly had an old hymn mixing with this new pop song until I had to Google the lyrics for both to separate them again. "There's Power in the Blood" has several verses, but the short version was summed up long ago in Philippians. We can do all things not because it's in our blood but because it's in His.

Giving up is in my blood just like it's in my daughter's and just like it's in everyone else's. We share that DNA as humans, and no nature or nurture can change it. But Jesus and His blood becomes ours and overwrites our genetic code, our predispositions, our weakness, and giving up is most certainly not in His blood.

I don't know what you're facing right now, but no matter what is in your path today or what's coming tomorrow, you can feel secure in the strength Jesus offers you. You can rest in the knowledge that giving up and giving in are not in His blood, and He's given us that power along with our salvation.

You can do this, whatever this is. You can stand up, you can fight back, you can hold on. Don't give up, friend. It isn't in His blood.

Dear God, I don't know if I can do this. This thing I'm facing feels like too much. It's too hard, too scary, too much! I know if I'm left to my own devices, I will never make it. Will You help me? Will You give me some of your strength? Will You help me face what's coming next—and do it with grace and peace and love? Just as Jesus faced the cross for the good of the resurrection and the people He loved so much, I know I must walk this path You've laid in front of me. For my good and Your glory, God, I know You're working it all together. Give me the strength to do my part. Thank You, God. Amen.

QUESTIONS TO CONSIDER

1. When you're faced with a difficult situation, are you tempted to rely on your own strength? Can you think of a time when your own strength failed you?

_____

_____

_____

_____

_____

_____

_____

2. What challenging circumstance are you facing right now? What is God calling you to today?

_____

_____

_____

_____

_____

_____

_____

3. How can you lean into His strength rather than relying on yourself? What do you need to ask Him for as you move forward?

_____

_____

_____

_____

_____

_____

_____

_____

DAY 40
PRAYER

Dear Lord,

What a journey this has been! I'm so grateful for this time set apart to seek You and find You, to draw near You and follow You. Though Easter will come and go, I will never stop appreciating your sacrifice and celebrating your resurrection. I will not forget your greatness or Your faithfulness, and I will not neglect seeking you. Please, Lord, don't let me forget You.

I know You've been refining me for a reason, God, and I know You have a plan for me. Please make it clear. Please open my eyes and my heart, and show me the next steps I should take. Show me how I can serve You right where I am, and show me exactly where You want me to go from here. Give me courage and give me wisdom as I follow You, give me a community of faith that can walk with me, and also give me humility to remember that You are the One making my paths straight.

Thank You, God—for loving me and forgiving me and ultimately, conquering sin and death for me. Thank You for everything. I love You.

Amen.

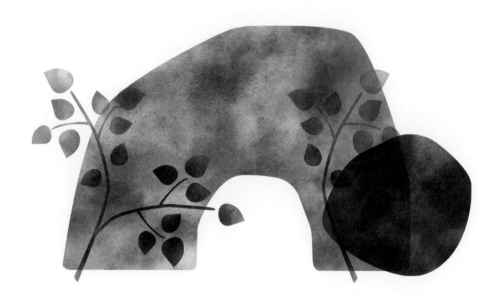

(in)courage welcomes you

to a place where authentic, brave women
connect deeply with God and others.
Through the power of shared stories and
meaningful resources, (in)courage champions
women and celebrates the strength Jesus gives
to live out our calling as God's daughters.
In the middle of your unfine moments and ordinary days,
you are invited to become a woman of courage.

Join us at **www.incourage.me** and
connect with us on social media!

@incourage

The **CSB (in)courage Devotional Bible** invites every woman to find her story *within the* greatest story ever told—God's story *of* redemption.

- **312 devotions** by 122 (in)courage community writers

- 10 distinct thematic **reading plans**

- Stories of courage from **50 women** of the Bible

- *and more features!*

Find out more at **incourageBible.com**

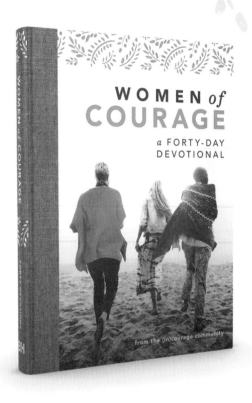

You are a Woman *of* Courage...
Because God says so.

Featuring 40 brave women from the Bible, this devotional will walk with you through the hardest days and leave you with the courage you need to lead, to love, to trust, and to turn to God in every situation.

Available now wherever books are sold.